The Displaced Person

by George Picart

the Peppertree Press

Sarasota, Florida

ISBN: 978-1-934246-62-7

Library of Congress Number: 2007927599

Printed in the U.S.A.

Printed June 2007

Dedicated to my parents,

Eugenie and Sergei Picart

To Kevin P. Donnelly
my Elks Friend

August 18, 2007

Acknowledgments

Loving thanks to my darling wife, Judy,
for countless hours of listening to my story.
Without her assistance and encouragement
to record all the details, the events in my
life story would not have been written.

A special thank you is also extended to
Gregory Jacob for his drawing on the cover.
He accurately captured my feelings as a displaced person

Foreword

This is the story about my courageous family and me, George Picart, who may have lost our homeland and material wealth but who never lost faith, hope, and love for one another. The primary reason for writing this story is to inform my descendents about the history of our ancestors. My words have been written in tribute of their courage and sacrifices, especially my Mom and Pop for their unwavering support, unflinching love, and positive influence. Their resilient spirit is deeply embedded in my mind and heart. I also hope that my book will inspire other displaced families in search of freedom and their quest to be dedicated and loyal American citizens.

For three generations, the evils of wars changed my family's life drastically; yet the will to live grew ever stronger. Faced with life threatening situations and heart wrenching decisions, many of my family members prevailed because of their bold decisiveness and courage. Their actions helped me learn that human beings can adapt when faced with agonizing struggles and that personal choices ultimately lead to life's adventures resulting in joys and/or sorrows. How and what we choose is vital to our destiny, and our choices affect our own lives and the lives of others, so ultimately we should try to choose wisely, yet choices can be based on a mere whim or dare, leading to wonderful results. At other times choices can be practical and safe, but results can be horrifying. Choices are rarely simple to make, but must be made, so individuals can survive and move on with life.

I have concluded that both the minor and major events in my family's life caused and affected our choices; yet interestingly, when others have encountered similar circumstances, the outcomes differed. These differences evoke discussions, debates, and more personal stories. Who or what guides us and why? Does God or a higher force intercede to help make us who we are and who we will become? These universal questions will continue to be pondered and debated. I will contribute my personal belief in the existence of little miracles that support our survival. Some may explain it simply as being in the right place at the right time. Whatever the explanation, my family and I finally settled in beautiful America, the land that accepted displaced refugees, and we had a chance to start a life, filled with positive expectations. I am forever grateful!

Picart Family

I t all started after Russia was defeated in the war with Turkey in 1878. The Russian Czar Alexander II hired foreign military officers from France, England, Germany, Sweden, and Poland to instruct the Russian Army in the latest military tactics, especially in the areas of discipline and modern warfare. My grandfather Jon Pierre Picart, from the southwest of France, was a captain in the French cavalry. As a young, single officer, Grandfather Picart, I surmise, was looking for adventure, so when he heard about the czar's offer for military advancement, he could not resist. He accepted the position as a cavalry instructor that included ownership of a house on a small estate in Kiev, the capital of Ukraine. At first, he communicated with the Russian soldiers in French, the language spoken by the educated officers, but then he began learning to converse in Russian, and his Russian friends affectionately addressed him as "Piotr," which is Peter.

As a handsome bachelor boasting the rank of major, Grandfather Picart mingled socially with other officers and their families joining them at festive parties, dances, and other recreational activities. The elite circle of upper-class military families seldom associated with civilians. At one of the dances, Grandfather Piotr met Elisabeth Kulikowicz, the daughter of an officer of Ukrainian descent. His charm and dancing skills captured Elisabeth's attention. They fell in love, married, and settled in Kiev. (Nowadays, Kiev is the capital of Ukraine, but when my grandparents lived there, it was part of the Russian Empire.) In Kiev they raised their two oldest sons, Alexander and Valentine. After a few years, the property in Kiev was sold because Grandfather was transferred to the military garrison in the city of Minsk, northwest of Kiev, and also part of the Russian Empire. (Nowadays Minsk is a city in Belarus, an independent country.)

My father, Sergius, who was their youngest son, was born on September 9, 1894, in Minsk. Interestingly, this was the same year that Czar Nicholas II Romanov began his reign as the last monarch of Russia. When Nicholas II came to the throne, people were starving because of several years of bad harvests. Most of the Russian people were poor, illiterate farmers or peasants who worked the land for the nobility. The peasants were too busy struggling to survive and not concerned with politics or ideas of revolution, but the workers in the industrialized cities were impatient for change. These new middle- or working-class Russians were more educated and politically informed. They were angry at the small group of Russian elite who splurged in luxurious wealth while most of the people lived in devastating poverty.

My father's family was not part of the nobility but a family that enjoyed the upper-class status of the military ranking, for Grandfather Picart was promoted to lieutenant colonel. Life in Minsk was contentment and prosperity for them, but unfortunately not for all of the Russian population.

In 1900 Grandfather Picart's regiment was ordered to the Manchurian border to fight in the Boxer Rebellion. His deployment was probably a concern to his family, the same fears and hardships that exist whenever those in the military are sent to fight in a foreign country. His regiment was actually part of the international fighting forces that consisted of Americans, Austrians, British, French, Germans, and Italians who squelched the Boxers, a group of militant Chinese who tried to evict foreigners from China by brutal killings. They were called Boxers because of the physical boxing and martial arts rituals that they practiced. The Boxer philosophy spread across northern China, instilling their creed of anti-Christian, anti-missionary, and anti-foreigners.

In one of the battles, Grandfather Jon Pierre Picart was killed. Ironically, a century later my daughter and her husband adopted a precious little girl, Li Ying (Maiya Grace) from China. What would the Boxers think about foreigners being invited to adopt Chinese babies?

Two years after Grandfather's death, Grandmother Elisabeth remarried another Russian officer, Ivan Petrovich Prigorowski, who was of Polish descent. He adopted her three sons, including my father. Each one of the sons became military officers, following the traditional careers of their father and stepfather. They attended a military school near Moscow in preparation for admittance to the Yaroslav Military Academy located northeast of Moscow. Each brother chose to specialize in different fields. The oldest son, Alexander, chose to be an engineer. The middle son, Valentine, selected one of the newest areas of study, aviation, completing two additional years of schooling. Following in his biological father's footsteps, my father joined the cavalry. Father disliked the military life, but obliged the tradition.

Prigorowski was a good husband and stepfather except for one weakness, overdrinking alcohol. As a veteran of the Boxer Uprising, he always recalled the excitement and horrors of his battle experiences. Drinking vodka was a way to comfort and ease his bad memories. At one of the parties, Captain Prigorowski overdrank and began proclaiming his dislike for the war strategies of Czar Nicholas II. He drew his revolver from his holster, aimed, and shot at the czar's portrait. Since he was a highly decorated war veteran, he was not court-martialed, but he was reprimanded and transferred to a less prestigious regiment in Vilnius, northwest of Minsk. Forced to sell their home in Minsk, the family purchased a house near the military post in Vilnius. Vilnius is now the capital city of Lithuania, yet when Prigorowski, Grandmother Elisabeth, and her sons moved there, the city was a province under Russian jurisdiction.

For a few years, the family and Captain Prigorowski lived a quiet, uneventful life, until one evening after lingering and drinking for many hours at the officer's club, Prigorowski commanded the orderly to drive him home. As the carriage approached a small bridge, the captain stood up and shouted, "Stop!" Prigorowski's confused thinking conjured up the fearful idea that the bridge was mined. Refusing to travel across, he foolishly proceeded to wade through the shallow brook to get to the other side, with water reaching to his chest at the deepest point. In the month of April, the water was not frozen, but bitter cold. He arrived home wet and shivering. The result of his actions led to the development of pneumonia and soon after caused his death.

Once again, Grandmother was a widow, but not for long. She was introduced to a widower, Charles Ronee, a military administrator living in Vilnius. He had no children from his first marriage, but they had three children: Anton, George, and Tanya. They continued to reside in Vilnius. My father, Sergius, was away at a military preparatory school when his older half-brother was born revealing a definite age gap between the new siblings. My calculations conclude that Grandmother Elisabeth began having more children when she was in her late thirties and early forties.

Father would often mention that Grandmother Elisabeth loved all her children and managed to keep the family happy no matter the hardships encountered. Singing and dancing were joys, and she seemed to always be crocheting. An only child of a military officer, she was accustomed to the military lifestyle of rules, regulations, and the horrors of wars, yet privileged to afford servants who helped with household chores. Soon after her first marriage, her parents died of minor illnesses due to the lack of medical knowledge. Fortunately, she was a strong woman in mind and body, who seemed to adapt and rise above difficult situations throughout her life.

While Grandmother was raising her second family, my father graduated from the military academy, was commissioned as a lieutenant, assigned to the Baltic Cavalry Regiment, and shipped to Helsinki, Finland. World War I was declared in 1914, and his regiment was part of the occupational forces to prevent the German Army from uniting with Finland, their probable ally. Stationed in Finland for three years until the Bolshevik Revolution in 1917, Father met Sonya, the daughter of a wealthy Finish businessman. She and her family befriended Father, inviting him to family functions, and he in turn included them as his guest at the dinner-dances held by the Russian officers. In fact, my father and Sonya were planning to become engaged, but as soon as word spread to Finland about the overthrowing of the czar's regime, the Russian troops rebelled. The officers were no longer in control and fled for safety. Realizing Father's dilemma, Sonya and her family sheltered and protected him from the raging Russian soldiers, assisting with the sale of his horse to obtain money to purchase civilian clothes and a ticket for passage on a ship heading back to his mother's home in Vilnius.

Every time my father recalled this time in Russia's history, he expressed feelings of confusion, for he had never mistreated his fellow soldiers no matter what their rank. He was raised in a strict military family with loyalty to the czar and the monarchy, always obeying rules and orders without question. Life under the czar's rule was superior for the officers compared to the poor peasants. He never realized their sufferings. Unfortunately, the eventual reign of communism enslaved everyone and saddened Father deeply.

When the Russians had to fight the Germans during the first year of World War I, the Russian military suffered severe casualties. The war impacted on Alexander, Father's eldest brother, who was captured by the Germans early on and spent most of the time as a POW in an officer's prison compound in a fortress somewhere in Prussia. Prisoners of War who were officers were treated with respect; for example, on several occasions he was able to visit with the German officers to socialize, enjoying privileges like playing chess and billiards. After Russia declared a cease-fire and signed the Treaty of Brest-Litovsk with Germany, he and the other prisoners were permitted to return home. Alexander was sent to Minsk, the location of his regiment's unit station. Though he had heard about the revolutionaries and the mistreatment of the czarist officers, he took a chance and returned to locate his fiancée. He believed that once proclaiming himself as a civilian, he would not be harmed; however, as soon as his identity was realized, he was arrested and sent to Kola Peninsula in northern Russia near the Arctic Sea where he died two years later because of brutal mistreatment by the communist guards. Grandmother Elisabeth learned that the guards drove spikes into the golden epaulets, piercing through the shoulders of those officers who wore their uniforms. Those few individuals who escaped relayed stories, depicting unbelievable brutality.

Valentine, Father's other brother, fared much better than Alexander. His war experiences involved the early stages of Russian aviation that was inferior to the Germans. He flew only one combat mission while he was stationed in Poland, another country that was a Russian province. Germans overran the airfield. Valentine was taken as a prisoner, and after the war he was released and returned unharmed to his family in Vilnius.

During the turmoil after the First World War, Poland was able to occupy Vilnius since the treaty enforced the Germans and Russians to retreat to their original borders, freeing Poland of their occupation. Poland's army marshal, Joseph Pilsuszki, the highest ranking general, who was also born in Vilnius, realized the opportunity to gain land from Lithuania and annexed the city of Vilnius and the surrounding territory for Poland, until 1939 when the Russians and Germans agreed to divide Poland once again.

After World War I, the two brothers, Valentine and Sergius Prigorowski (Picart), and their stepsiblings, the Ronees, along with their mother Elisabeth and stepfather Charles Ronee, adapted to their new life in Vilnius under Polish reign. Valentine married Frieda, a Jewish girl, who converted to Russian Orthodox. His first job was driving a bus. Since he was mechanically inclined and an industrious worker, he decided to purchase and rebuild an old bus, starting his own private bus line that traveled to the outskirts of Vilnius. The Ronee children prospered with their lives. After graduating from the University of Vilnius, Anton became a civil engineer. George, the younger brother, also attended the university, but dropped out to become a railroad conductor. Tanya, their sister, became a medical secretary for a Jewish gynecologist, Dr. Lewes, whom she later married. The family members established themselves in the community. Life went on.

Fuchs Family
Maternal Grandparents

On October 1, 1869, Otto Albert Julius Fuchs was born in Benbeniki, East Prussia, to a wealthy and influential business family, actively involved in the government of the (German) Kaiser monarchy. Grandfather Fuchs served as a senator for East Prussia and held a prominent position as an officer of telegraph communications.

He married Emma Louise Maria Von Bretenstein, born on December 27, 1869, in Smolensk, Russia. She was also from an affluent Prussian family. Eventually, the young couple moved to Vilnius because of Grandfather's promotion to superintendent of telegraph. Grandfather's prestigious position for directing communications throughout the Lithuanian province was a vital service to the residents. Operations flourished, and he purchased property and built a three-story house that included a ballroom accommodating one hundred people. His wealth derived not only from earnings from his employment but also from family inheritances. Grandfather also received a hoffrat's (senator's) pension for the rest of his life.

His wife Emma Louise bore four daughters and a son. Before World War I, he and his family relocated temporarily to Moscow by request of the Russian government to modernize their telegraph system. Olga and Lida, the eldest daughters, began working in the telegraph operations as well in Russia. The youngest daughters, Helena and Eugenie, my mother, went to school in Moscow. Their brother, who was the baby of the family, died when he was six years old from scarlet fever.

In 1917 while the family resided in Moscow, the Russian revolutionaries rebelled against the rule of Russian Czar Nicholas II, resulting in the downfall of the Russian monarchy, and Vladimir Lenin and the Bolsheviks (Communists and the Red Army) came to power forming the foundation for the Soviet Union. Complete chaos emerged in Moscow as a result of lack of supplies, especially food. Mother was merely fifteen years old at the time and later recalled standing on line for hours to obtain small rations of bread and vegetables. She was concerned about her family, particularly worried about the health of her mother, so she would lie and tell everyone that she had eaten her portion of the rations on the way home. To alleviate her nagging hunger pains, she would dissolve rock-sugar in her mouth while drinking cups of tea. This poor diet went on for weeks resulting in malnutrition and the shrinkage of her intestines. Grandfather Fuchs and his family had duel citizenship as Germans and Lithuanians and since he still owned property in Vilnius, they were finally permitted to leave Moscow. Their return was just in time, for Eugenie needed immediate medical attention that was available in the excellent hospital in Vilnius, where she underwent surgery to replace sections of her intestines with goat intestines. She recovered and never had any intestinal ailments for the rest of her life. One of my mother's vivid memories of a time in Moscow was a farewell dinner she and the family attended prior to returning to Lithuania. They were also given packages of pastries for their long trip by train. The amount of food, suddenly available, was unbelievable!

Not returning with the family, Olga and Lida decided to stay in Moscow for another year. Why they made that decision, I am not sure, but I surmise that they had boyfriends and wanted to remain with them. When they finally wanted to leave, the Communist government closed the borders, not allowing anyone to enter or exit. Years later, they married and had children. My mother received letters from her sisters, but the contents of the letters contained general information with careful wording because the government officials censored all communications. One of my cousins was a pilot in the USSR air force. No further information is known about my relatives in Russia.

Life in Vilnius

Vilnius, an ancient city with an extensive history rich in cultural, commercial, and educational experiences, continues to be a prominent city and the capital of Lithuania, however, in1918 Poland regained territory and controlled Vilnius. The city was renamed Wilno.

When my father finally located his mother and remaining family in Vilnius (Wilno), he decided to settle there and find employment. He tried various jobs, but none were challenging, until he began working for a company that vulcanized rubber tires and tubes. Since the need for rubber products was growing, his job became a lucrative endeavor, especially with the surge of automobile sales causing rubber to become an important and demanding commodity for the future. Researching and studying the possibilities to enhance in this line of work, Father was convinced that starting his own business would prove to be profitable as well as interesting. He worked hard to strive for this dream.

When Father was not working, he became involved with the Russian Czarist Officers Club in Vilnius (Wilno), where he mingled with former czarist officers and their families who fled from communism. The club members not only met for social functions to renew old acquaintances, but also raised funds to start a private school for their children, so the Russian language and culture could be proudly taught and perpetuated. They wanted to continue the legacy of the czarist era.

Years after the Russian Revolution, Father had contacted a former czarist officer, a cavalry captain, who was living in Paris. During and after the revolution, many czarist officers fled to France since they could speak French and communicating in a familiar language would make relocation easier. Father had seen his friend's name in a White-Russian newspaper that was printed in France and published by former czarist officers. Since Father had no mementos of his past life as an officer, the captain sent a copy of a booklet, a cherished keepsake, about the history of the Yaroslav Military Academy where they had attended school. I enjoy reading its contents, not only to absorb the interesting information, but also to practice reading in Russian. One fact is that the academy was established in the ninth century, and many of its graduates were spread apart throughout the world. Father fondly remembered the camaraderie and friendships established when he was at the academy. The students formed a close bond that lasted as long as they lived. Perhaps this proud allegiance was one of the reasons that my father and the other czarist officers in Vilnius (Wilno) tried to preserve the history of the Russian Empire through the establishment of the Russian Officers Club, an important way to fulfill their goal.

Elite citizens of Vilnius who were not Russian also patronized and participated in the various functions sponsored by the club. Formal balls, including vocal and instrumental performances, were enjoyed by all. At one of these social events, Sergius Prigorowski (Picart), my father, met Eugenie Fuchs, my mother. He courted her for about a year, and they were married on October 25, 1926, the ninth anniversary of the October Revolution in Russia, when the armed workers took control of Petrograd (St. Petersburg), capturing Czar Nicholas II and his family at their Winter Palace. A year later on September 4, 1927, I was born.

Father continued working in the rubber vulcanizing business, and finally with the financial help from Grandfather Fuchs, he opened his own business. At first all the machinery was steam driven, but eventually he improved the machinery converting the plant to electrical power, making production cleaner and more efficient. He also created various molds for other items made of rubber like balls, dolls, and an assortment of toys. Receiving a medal from the city for one of the most modern and advanced plants was an incentive to continue plans for further technological developments and kept Father very busy.

For the next twelve years, my life and my family's life in Vilnius (Wilno) would be wonderful. Vilnius was not only my birthplace but also my beloved home. Even though I attended a private Russian school, the Polish language was mandated as the primary language, but Russian was my most fluent language. Father and Mother stressed the importance of education. I recall walking two miles to school with my friend, George Sipailo, who was also a son of a former czarist officer. There were no such things as snow days. I bundled-up, left early, and walked quickly to be sure I would arrive on time.

All the students wore uniforms. A boy's uniform consisted of a white shirt and blue tie, underneath a navy blue, long-sleeved jacket with light blue piping trimming the cuffs. Three brass buttons fastened it closed, and a patch on the left side had the inscription, A.S. Pushkin School. The school was named after the famous Russian author, Alexander Sergaiovicz Pushkin. A light blue stripe adorned each side of the navy blue pants. A symbol on top of an open book with the number four, designating School Number 4, was on a pea cap worn by the boys. Each girl wore a white blouse, blue skirt and jacket, with the same patch on the sleeve, and a beret with a pin of an open book with the number of the school.

In each classroom, the girls and boys were separated, with one side of the room for girls and the other side for the boys. Only female teachers taught my classes, and they were extremely strict. They walked around the room with a ruler that was used to tap or strike students who did not sit straight in their seats, misbehaved, or daydreamed.

I loved school and enjoyed learning. My favorite subjects were geography and history. I remember the numerous homework drills to learn Polish and Russian. The two languages with completely different alphabets were a challenge to master at the same time. Today, I am fluent in Russian and Polish, as well as German and English, and some French and Lithuanian, which I seem to have difficulty speaking because of little use. Practice does make perfect.

Russian authors, Lev Tolstoy, Alexander Pushkin, Lermantov, and Dostojewski were required readings. I also very much enjoyed reading the American comic books, translated into Polish. Once a month, I would run to the kiosk or newsstand to purchase a comic with the latest episode of Flash Gordon, depicting space travel and rocket ships landing on the Moon and Mars. Father would be critical of this fantasy reading and tell me to read non-fiction books. Years later, when jet planes were invented, he voiced his regrets about discouraging the reading of comic books, admitting that anything was possible.

The school's curriculum included athletics. Soccer, hockey, and ice-skating were the sports I most enjoyed playing. Of course, sportsmanship was absolutely enforced. A player would never strike an opposing contender intentionally, and if an opponent were down, he would be helped up. Fair competition was emphasized. Music and art classes were also encouraged. When I was in the fourth grade, I joined the Balalaika Ensemble, playing at school performances. The balalaika is a triangular-shaped musical instrument, similar to a mandolin and ukulele. Each balalaika performer was dressed like a Cossack in a black fur hat, called a "papacha," a white, silk shirt with long, puffed sleeves and a high-buttoned neckline, red pants, and black boots.

During the summer, I always looked forward to family excursions to the beach on the Vilejka River. About two blocks from my house, a paddleboat, approximately one hundred feet long, took passengers five miles up the river to a sandy beach that stretched out for at least two miles. My father made special rubber toys to be used in the water. One favorite toy was a huge ball with handles, and another was a ring, similar to a tire tube. It was fun playing and floating with these water toys. Father and I knew how to swim, but Mother never learned. She was afraid to swim in the river and waded in the water or sat in the sun, mostly underneath the umbrella to protect her fair skin from sunburn. Mother would beckon us to join her on the beach to eat the delicious food she had prepared. As she would empty the straw basket filled with scrumptious treats, we knew she was a loving mother and wife, always concerned about nourishing our bodies. As a matter of fact, she asked our family doctor what foods would make me strong and healthy. He suggested feeding me chicken, so that is what I ate nearly everyday. Needless to say, chicken is not one of my favorite meats.

Visiting Grandfather and Grandmother Fuchs, who lived on the south side near the outskirts of Vilnius where there were beautiful parks and pine forests, was fun for everyone. On three acres of land, my grandparents' house and property were huge. Each room was enormous with ceilings twelve feet high, a full apartment downstairs with a dance hall, and another apartment upstairs with the same number of rooms and dance hall.

The Fuchs loved to entertain and invite friends and family to splendid parties with music being played on two grand pianos, one in each hall. Helena, their youngest daughter, attended the Music Conservatory and became a piano instructor. She enjoyed playing at her parent's gala parties. Dancing was an important part of the festivities. The waltz, polka, tango, fox trot, and mazurka were favorite dances.

Adjacent to the house was the servants' quarters, which later became a storage facility. In the backyard, a gazebo overlooked a magnificent garden of fruit trees and bushes with all sorts of berries for making wine, Grandfather's favorite hobby. His homemade wine came in many flavors like loganberry, strawberry, and the one I liked to sample, raspberry. The wines were sweet, fragrant, and delicious! He also made a rice wine. After the fermentation of the wine, it was strained. Then sugar and a little bit of water was fried in a pan until it looked like a golden syrup. The syrup was mixed with the fermented wine, transforming its color from white to a light shade of gold. The family longed to taste his creation. I was usually permitted to sample a small amount of each wine and felt privileged to be given this special treat.

Since Grandfather Fuchs was retired from the telegraph business and his position as senator, he not only devoted his time to winemaking, but also to serving as a member of the Lutheran Church Council. He was not only a respected citizen of Vilnius (Wilno), but also an excellent role model. He was strict, but fair and good hearted.

I recall admiring photographs of Grandfather in his formal uniform, with a decorative sword hanging from his side, worn when he was the superintendent of telegraphs. It was the custom that government employees wear uniforms that were similar to the military; however, the colors and insignias were different, coinciding with the department represented. When he showed me his gold-plated sword, I was impressed, and he promised to give it to me when I was older. I could not wait to possess that magnificent weapon since it belonged to my magnificent grandfather.

Aunt Helena, my mother's youngest sister, lived in the first floor apartment of Grandfather's house with her husband, Eugene Gryzuto, who had been a Russian czarist infantry officer and was employed in the city's tax collecting office. They had married a year after my parents and had one child, Alexandria, who was born on July 7, 1929. Whenever I visited my grandparents, Alexandria and I became playmates. Riding bicycles was one of our favorite past times. Since Grandmother was sickly, having Helena living nearby was a perfect arrangement for she could help her ailing mother. Years later, Grandmother's illness was diagnosed as cancer, and she eventually passed away on July 4, 1943. Grandfather died on July 13, 1947.

One of my fondest memories was wintertime in Vilnius (Wilno), when my family would visit family and friends. We rode in a horse-driven sleigh, because the snow was too deep for cars. All taxis stopped operating, and sleds were used instead. The snowfall usually started in early October accumulating on the average to around five feet or more. Mounds of snow lasted until spring and sometimes until the month of May. Visions of horse driven plows and men shoveling snow on the streets and onto huge sleds and hauling the snow to the river where it was dumped are vivid. I loved the snow! Building snow castles, competing in snowball fights, sleigh riding, skiing, and ice skating were lots of fun. It was a glorious time!

Most enjoyable was Christmas. I was fortunate to celebrate two Christmases, since my mother was Lutheran, and the birth of Jesus was based on the Gregorian calendar on December 25, and a second celebration with my father's parents coincided with the Julian calendar for the Russian Orthodox religion. We would attend midnight service. Riding to church in a horse-driven sleigh was exhilarating. Since the temperature was minus-thirty degrees Fahrenheit, our bodies were tucked under bearskin blankets as our sleigh sped over the frozen road. The joyful jingles of the bells around the horse's neck; the rhythmic crunches of the frozen snow under the horse's hooves; and the occasional cracks of the driver's whip in the frosty air alerted my senses to thrills of excitement. When our sleigh slowed, we heard the voices of the Christmas carolers from the neighborhood, and we began singing, too, voices mingling.

My memory is vivid. Starting several days before Christmas Eve, the preparation for the holidays was hard work. The women baked and cooked everything from scratch. Delicious aromas permeated throughout the house. Always wearing an apron, Mother stood at the kitchen table, surrounded by all kinds of spices and ingredients ready to create holiday treats. Chopping vanilla sticks and an assortment of nuts and raisins to blend into a batter of butter cookies, poppy seed loaves, babkas, and various pastries was like watching a production line in a factory. My mouth watered for pickled and breaded herring filet in tomato sauce. Not wasting anything, left over meat was ground and blended with hard boiled eggs, sautéed onions, and a multitude of spices to be spread onto a special dough, rolled to resemble a loaf of bread and then baked until the crust was golden brown. The fragrance of this delicious concoction was delightfully yummy. I still make this special meat filling surrounded by a flaky pastry crust. It is scrumptious!

The Christmas celebration lasted for three days. Stores and schools closed. Friends and family visited one another, exchanging gifts, sampling foods, chatting vociferously, and admiring decorations. Holidays were a festive, joyous time for everyone seemed jolly.

The Christmas tree in our parlor was about twelve feet high. I played endlessly with the train set under the tree. Mother always knew where to find me. I often think back in amazement that the burning candles adorning the tree did not cause a fire. There must have been over a hundred candles on the tree. Each candle was securely pushed into a bowl-shaped holder with a clip on the side, which in turn was attached to a branch. Decorations made of paper, wood, and glass sat on the branches as well. Father would light each candle with another candle attached to a long pole. Being cautious, he only lit the candles when we sat in the parlor usually after dinner. When the candles were not lit, spotlights shined on the tree. Eventually, electric lights were available and much safer. Our Christmas tree would stay up longer and not be taken down until after the Feast of the Three Kings, signifying the celebration of the Russian Orthodox Christmas. I loved every moment!

I credit Father for telling me the history of our family. We would sit together for many hours talking or playing chess, which he felt was an important game to learn for it developed brain cells that improved thinking skills. I often marvel about Father's positive attitude about life. No matter what catastrophe, he never became emotional or despairing. He would reiterate that his love for Mother and our family was strong enough to overcome any misery or hardship encountered. Father continues to be an inspirational role model for my brother and me.

Mother also adored her family and was strong minded. She had many interests including a special hobby. She loved dogs. After having a large heated building erected at the back of our property, she decided to raise Dobermans. She was able to obtain a brown, male Doberman from Germany. This dog was a pedigree with certified credentials as a pure bred Doberman. She then purchased a black, female Doberman from Sweden also with pedigree documents. Lora was the female, and Pasha was the male. Their first litter consisted of dogs that were black and brown, but the second litter emerged with one dog that was black, one that was a silver male, and all the other puppies were brown. When this second litter was about a week old, I watched while Lora allowed her pups to suckle her milk, but I walked too close to the pup, and Lora jumped up and bit me on the head and shoulder. I think that the dog would have killed me, if Mother had not been nearby. I was rushed to our family doctor and he patched me up.

Mother's hobby expanded into a small business, because Dobermans were in demand. She sold all the puppies except the silver male. He became my pet, and I named him Prince. When Prince was sent to the veterinarian to trim his ears and tail, I cried all day. I knew he would be hurting. After obedience school, Prince was a one-man dog. He would not accept food from anyone but me. Wherever I went, Prince would follow, walking right beside me. He rarely barked, but if he felt that I was threatened or in danger, he merely growled and showed his teeth, and his actions would scare away the meanest bully. Soon after, Mother acquired another brown, female Doberman who mated with Prince. The result was one brown and five silver Dobermans. A family acquaintance came to visit and said he would pay whatever the price, but Mother was more interested in finding each dog a good home. The money she made covered the cost of breeding expenses with a small profit for her.

Visiting Grandma Elizabeth, Father's mother, who lived on the north side of Vilnius (Wilno), was just as much fun as visiting my other grandparents. On Sundays, her children and their families would be invited for dinner. Uncle George was my buddy, playing chess, checkers and card games together. During the summer, Uncle Valentine would take me along on his job as a bus driver. After dropping the passengers off at the end of the route, a scheduled layover wait of about an hour and a half or sometimes two hours before the return trip home, usually allowed for lots of leisure time. We would eat lunch with an added ice cream treat for me. I would watch Uncle Valentine play billiards, which was our secret, since his wife Frieda objected to his playing pool for money. She was right. He lost more than he won.

Yes, my life in Vilnius (Wilno) was nearly perfect until Sunday, September 3, 1939, the day before my twelfth birthday. The weather was beautiful, sunny and bright. Grandma Elisabeth was expecting us for dinner and ready to serve a special birthday cake for dessert in honor of my birthday. It was almost like any other Sunday, except for the fact that Mother was five months pregnant and did not feel well enough to attend the family dinner. She stayed home to rest. Father and I decided to walk the two miles to Grandmother Elisabeth's house instead of driving. We talked as we walked about the radio report that the German troops were being deployed on the Polish border. I was not concerned for I thought the war would be far away from us, but Father seemed somewhat worried about the future; yet he did not dwell over his anxieties because he wanted me to have a happy day.

It was around noon, and we were approximately four blocks from our destination, when suddenly air raid sirens began blaring. Father jokingly said, "Well, the town is testing the air raid sirens. Let's hope they work and give us enough warning to protect ourselves in case the Germans attack."

We continued walking and talking about the terrible consequences of war, when we heard airplanes overhead. The next sounds were explosions and screams. Grabbing my arm, Father pulled me across the street underneath the protection of an arched entranceway of a large building. Diagonally across from us, I saw a house ripped apart from the blast of a bomb. Even though I felt Father's strong arms hugging me close to his body, I trembled in fear. I put my head between his arm and chest, hiding my face, but I could still hear the loud explosions.

Later on, we learned that the Germans had bombed a railroad station a few miles away. Bombs strayed, hitting and destroying homes and innocent people. When the sirens blew an all-clear signal, we ran to Grandmother's house. Everyone was upset, but there was no damage or injuries. Anxiously, we started home, encountering mass confusion on the way. Frantic people were rushing everywhere. Others slowly walked in a daze, and some sobbed and cried hysterically. The city was in complete turmoil. There was no transportation. Buses and taxis stopped. We could not get a ride. Finally arriving home, thank God, Mother and our house were safe.

After the bombings, Vilnius (Wilno) was in a state of war, yet life went on. Students attended classes. Citizens returned to work and transportation resumed. The only difference was the presence of the Polish military everywhere. Soldiers patrolled the streets. There were no further attacks on the city by the Germans, but we expected them to occupy Vilnius (Wilno) at any moment; however, surprisingly the Soviet Army marched into the city and quickly without resistance took over complete control. The Polish soldiers were captured, and years later, we learned that many were killed by the Russians.

A month later, Vilnius (Wilno) was no longer a Polish territory but a Lithuanian province under Russian control and renamed Vilnius. Ironically, history repeats itself, for during the reign of the Russian Empire, Lithuania was also a province of Russia. Lithuanians headed the government and all the institutions. In school, the Lithuanian teachers were hired to teach the subjects in the Lithuanian language, and Russian was mandated as the second language.

It is indescribable to convey the difficulties encountered by the people. Poland ceased to exist because the country was divided between Germany and Russia in a devious plan between Hitler and Stalin that allowed the Soviet Union to annex and control the eastern part of Poland, where we lived, as well as Lithuania, Latvia, and Estonia. Since Vilnius originally was the capital of Lithuania, the Russians permitted the Lithuanians to use Vilnius as their capital once again but under complete Russian control. Lithuanian police were transferred to Vilnius, yet the Russian military was the occupational force. The Polish population and other nationalities in Vilnius lost their identity and were forced to become Lithuanians. Money was changed to Lithuanian currency. Names of the streets were changed. The name of the capital was changed from the Polish word Wilno back to Vilnius.

Life changed drastically! Food, fuel, clothes, and most essentials were unavailable. The Russians confiscated everything. Waiting in line for hours, the small amounts of food for sale were rationed. First come, first served was the policy. Bakeries ran out of bread by noontime. The food shortage was terrible and reminded Mother of the food shortages she and her family had experienced in 1917 when they had lived in Moscow.

A personal devastation was the confiscation of Father's rubber business. He was no longer the owner, but hired to work for the Red Army in his own factory, vulcanizing mostly their military equipment and providing the Russians with his expertise and supplies. Other businesses and factories were completely dismantled and sent to Russia. There were no choices in the matter. The Russian forces ruled. If the Soviet authorities needed anything at anytime, it would be taken and used at their discretion. Freedom with choices was over. Life was miserable! I cannot remember celebrating Christmas in 1939.

Mother began her ninth month of pregnancy in January of 1940. As usual, each day she would walk to the doghouse and feed the Dobermans. On one particular day, one of the dogs was so excited to see her that he jumped at her stomach and knocked her down. Even though Mother was in some pain, she picked herself up and continued her chores. Later she felt better and was not concerned, but on the twentieth of January, she went into labor and surprisingly delivered twins. My brother, Alexander was born healthy, but his twin sister was stillborn. Losing a baby that she did not realize she was carrying was shockingly sad, but Mother decided to focus her attention on her healthy baby boy. For me, it was strange to have a little brother joining our family, but I adjusted and sincerely enjoyed having him around. Alex's birth was not only a blessing, but also a pleasant diversion from the hard times we faced.

Food shortages worsened! Providing food for the Dobermans was difficult, so Mother sadly decided to give away her beautiful dogs. A local farmer who delivered dairy products to our house showed interest in the dogs. She gave away all of them except for Prince, my beloved pet. Unfortunately, one of the Russian soldiers would see Prince and me visiting Father at work. The soldier demanded that I give him Prince. I explained and argued and pleaded that Prince was my dog, but the soldier did not care. Muzzled and leashed, Prince was taken away. I cried for days and days.

In the spring of 1940, a delegation from the German government came to Vilnius to repatriate the people of German descent. At the same time a Soviet colonel, who was in charge of confiscated properties and who had befriended Father, approached him with a confidential suggestion to leave Vilnius as soon as possible because the Russian elite secret police, the KGB, would most likely discover that Father had been a czarist officer. The colonel warned Father, because he had respected his rank as a fellow military officer. His kind act saved Father from being sent to Siberia or worse being killed.

Upon learning about the possible disclosure of Father's past service as a czarist officer, Grandfather Fuchs took action. Being a notable Prussian citizen, he registered his entire family to be included as part of the repatriation to Germany. Even though his two sons-in-law were not German, they and their families acquired German passports. The repatriation train for those who were of German heritage was scheduled to leave Vilnius in a week, yet we had to pretend that we were not planning to leave. Most of the time Father hid at a friend's house in case the Russians came in search of him, and the rest of us did not pack anything in advance, so as not to create suspicion.

Meeting Father at the train station the morning of departure, we carried only two suitcases containing our most important and needed belongings. Everything else was left behind. I did not mind leaving my toys, the train set, comic books, and other materialistic things because I began to learn at a young age that survival and being with those you love are the most important possessions in your life.

The Russian guards inspected everyone boarding the train, checking to be sure that proper German credentials were submitted. At that time the Russians were trying to be courteous and obliging to all those with German passports. We were fortunate to escape the Communist regime.

Father's family, left in Vilnius, was not so lucky. Six months after our departure, Uncle Valentine was arrested because of his past affiliation as a czarist officer and sent to Siberia where he was incarcerated for ten years. In the summer of 1941, Germany attacked Russia and controlled and occupied Vilnius, enabling Father to send and receive mail to his family. Grandmother Elisabeth and he communicated often until the beginning of 1944, when the Russians gained control of Vilnius once again. At that time, Grandmother Elisabeth, her three Ronee offsprings, and Aunt Frieda, Valentine's wife, were forced to relocate to Kiev for the rest of their lives. Ironically, Grandmother was returning to the place of her birth, but not under happy circumstances. Olga, Grandmother's widowed and childless sister-in-law, continued living with her. They had lived together in Vilnius ever since Grandmother's husband, Charles Ronee, had died. She and Grandmother were best friends. After relocating to Kiev, Olga passed away and Grandmother Elisabeth never remarried. She was one hundred and three years old when she died.

Some Russian families followed the custom of photographing a dead relative laid out in a coffin. I have Grandmother's picture at her wake surrounded by the three Ronee siblings, other relatives, and Uncle Valentine who survived his ordeal in Siberia. To some people it may be a gruesome photograph, but for me I see a delicately featured and elegant lady who strikingly resembles the beautiful grandmother I knew so many years ago. I am proud to be one of her descendants.

Leaving Vilnius was not only an emotionally sad time and financial loss for my family, but also a painful move for Grandfather Fuchs. He not only left property, treasures, and wealth behind, but also cherished friends and a home he loved for many years. Grandfather had planned to be buried in the magnificent mausoleum he had built for himself and the whole family. It was constructed of imported Italian marble. When he died after the war, he was buried in a pine box, instead of an ornate casket, in an ordinary plot in a cemetery in Urfahr, Austria. Admirably without hesitation, Grandfather chose the safety of his family over possessions and materialistic glory. I salute gratefully and acknowledge proudly his loving sacrifices for his family's safety. Thank you, Grandfather, for teaching me one of life's important lessons.

Austria

Apanproximately three to four hundred families, in similar circumstances, traveled southwest on the train. We were labeled the *Volks Deutsche*, which means folks of German descent. Our first stop was outside Thorn (Poland) that was now occupied by Germans. We were taken to a huge castle near the Wisla River. This great river divides Poland from south to north, and the capital city of Warshawa is on its bank. We lived in the castle for one month. Accommodations were similar to a dormitory with separate rooms for men and women. Each room housed sixty bunk beds. Since I was older, I slept in a bunk bed above Father, and my infant brother stayed with Mother. It was very strange sleeping in a room with so many people.

Families dined together in a huge hall and socialized after meals. Exploring the beautiful grounds around the castle that was on the top of a hill would lead me to the Wisla River about a half of a mile away. Because it was spring, I would run and walk over the grass-covered land, stopping to pick or smell the numerous wild flowers in bloom. The surroundings seemed almost too peaceful and perfect. We thought of our stay at Thorn as a vacation while awaiting assignment for our next destination. At times it was boring with no school or work, so Father and I would venture to the city discovering more medieval architecture.

At last, we were moved to Asten, a village approximately five miles east of Linz, Austria, and about a mile from the Danube River. We were herded into a huge camp with fifty barracks. Each barrack had thirty rooms with two washrooms with showers, one for females and the other for males. Rest rooms were also separated by gender. A large kitchen with many coal stoves was the only area for cooking meals. Each family occupied one room with four bunk beds, a small table, four chairs, and a metal chest. Larger families were assigned an additional room. *Volks Deutche* from other German occupied countries resided in this camp, until the completion of processing designated families to different locations in Austria or Germany. The German officials in charge determined destinations.

While at this camp, everyone received small rations of food and supplies. Families began adjusting to camp life, following rules and regulations and accepting all directives and decisions. Religious services were not allowed within the camp, and the churches were far away, so we gathered as a family to pray for strength, guidance, and continued togetherness. It was strange, yet a tolerable living situation. After two months, we were transferred to a smaller camp in Austria on the northern outskirts of Linz, a mile from the Danube River. We lived there until the end of the Second World War in 1945.

These barracks were similar in formation to the previous facilities, but this time there were only a total of twelve barracks. *Umsiedlungs Lager Auhof* was the name of the camp, which stood for "Displaced Persons Camp in Auhof." The camp, surrounded by mountains with an abundance of trees, shrubs, and flowers, provided scenic views and some nourishing food. On the lush bushes grew an assortment of berries, and the undergrowth of the forest supplied edible mushrooms. One of my favorite mushrooms was called the egg mushroom, brown and oval shaped. When cooked, it had a distinct taste that enhanced the flavor of any meal. I still enjoy cooking and eating all sorts of mushrooms.

Men between the ages of eighteen and forty-five were drafted into the German Army. Thank God, Father was over the age limit, and of course I was not yet fourteen. Older men like Father were assigned jobs in the city, so Father worked in a steel mill that produced tanks for the military. Mother constantly prayed for Father's safe return, since the mill was bombed daily. Dashing into the bunker, Father beat death many times. During one bombing, the section of the building where Father would usually be working was totally destroyed. Cleaning up debris and rebuilding sections of the structures were ongoing.

With daily air raids, no one could rest or be caught off guard. Mother was prepared for each emergency. Alex's carriage was packed with food, clothes, blankets, bottles, and diapers, ready for a run into the bomb shelter. Mother slept in her clothes, not to waste any time. The siren would begin to blare and Mother and Alex were off on a race to safety. Barely five feet tall, her short legs would resemble a sandpiper running on the beach scurrying away from an oncoming wave. Because of her conscientious organization and swiftness, she made it to the air raid shelter before anyone else.

Life was sad with little time for fun activities because of the constant alert to survive from dangers. Shortages in all areas made life even more difficult. Concentrating on basic needs was an ordeal. Hunger consumed our strength, weakening not only our bodies, but also our minds. Rations of food were meager, hardly enough to satisfy or nourish. A weekly ration per person consisted of one egg, eight ounces of meat, a loaf of bread, a pint of milk, a half of a stick of butter, and two to three ounces of cooking oil. Potatoes and cabbage were staple foods. Each family attempted to grow small gardens of cucumbers, beans, radishes, and anything else to eat. As a teenager, I recall always being hungry. We would pray together as often as we could to thank God and remind one another that we were safe and were still together, but at times we thought God was too busy to hear our prayers.

Mere existence is depressing, so attending school lifted my spirits and occupied my mind most of the time. Walking a mile and a half to the bus stop on the main road in Linz, the other children and I boarded the public bus to attend the local school that was about five miles from the camp. On one occasion walking home from the bus stop without realizing, I had crossed over an unexploded time bomb. That bomb went off one hour later. We heard the explosion at the camp. When I strolled along the same path the next day, to my horror, I saw a huge hole in the road. It was the exact spot I had crossed the previous day. Often the school day was interrupted or canceled due to bombing. Although the planes usually targeted strategic points, the bombs would stray and explode on civilian property. My family and I considered our selves very fortunate to have been spared from severe harm.

My school years in Linz were challenging because I had to master the German language, especially the difficult grammar. To improve my language skills which were not sufficient to attend the next level of higher education, I was put back a year. In Europe there were two types of high school. One was the *Ober Schuhle* for general education, and the other school was called the *Gymnasium* for students pursuing further education in preparation for a professional career requiring entrance to a university. I will never forget the time when I first arrived in America, filling out my job application. One section inquired about my education, and I recorded that I had completed elementary school and the gymnasium. My words caused much laughter to my embarrassment, until I realized that in America, a gymnasium is the physical education room and not the name for high school.

During the summer, each student was required to attend a boot camp, where instructors devised activities to enhance military tactics and experiences. Groups were formed to participate in military exercises and games with a specific goal to perhaps capture an opponent's flag or a specific area. Utilizing camouflage to hide in the terrain, reading maps, using a compass, and practicing other drills were enforced. Fun events were also included to help form friendships. I especially enjoyed the sing-a-longs around the campfire to promote a more relaxed atmosphere.

Volunteering to work on a farm, a hospital, or at any other facility of civic need was also a school requirement. The youth were too busy to get into trouble, until it was my turn in the summer of 1943 to attend one of the camps located in Postlingberg on the property of a prestigious farmer where I met another student, Steffie. She was one of several girls, who volunteered to complete all sorts of chores on the farm. I was one, of a group of one hundred boys, who was scheduled to participate in four weeks of camp activities, emphasizing military exercises. Away from the farmhouse, the boys stayed in a huge building that contained a kitchen, dining room, washroom with showers, and sleeping quarters. We were not aware of the girls' presence.

After lunch on Sunday, all the students had time off. On my very first Sunday, I decided to explore the farm. That is the time when I first met

Steffie, sitting on a bench outside the farmhouse. We chatted and were immediately attracted to one another. Agreeing to meet again the next day after dinner, we held hands and kissed, and before we knew it, we had planned a secret rendezvous at ten o'clock when everyone was asleep. That night, Steffie quietly tiptoed into the boy's building and joined me in the washroom, where high expectations for our first sexual experience fizzled. Two virgins trying to figure out the right position resulted in loud noises that awakened the female cook who decided to investigate the commotion. When she opened the door, switched on the light, and discovered two half naked bodies in a clutch on the floor, we knew we were in trouble. Jumping up, Steffie escaped to the farmhouse, and I ran back to my room. The cook did not follow, but I knew she would report what she had witnessed. I spent a sleepless night worrying about the consequences of my actions.

The next day after breakfast, I was called into the commander's office. It was not a pleasant experience. I was discharged and sent home immediately. I found out later that Steffie was reprimanded and not permitted to have any sort of contact with the males at the camp. A copy of the report explaining my unfavorable and shameful conduct was sent to my parents. Mother was upset, but Father's comments were more casual, emphasizing that my actions were merely a sign that I was growing up. His easygoing manner was typical of his philosophy on life. Not many things surprised him, and if he was concerned or worried he rarely showed it. Did I learn my lesson? I was scared away from girls for quite a while!

For the remainder of the summer, I was reassigned to help the workers in a basket-weaving factory, spending several hours each day in a field stripping the rushes to be woven into baskets. It was a boring job, but I stayed out of trouble and was glad when it was time to return to school.

All males and females between the ages of nine and seventeen were mandated to be in the Hitler Youth Organization, which encouraged pride in one's German heritage. Daily meetings were held after school and often on weekends. Uniforms were required when attending any function. I was forced to be a part of this organization, because I attended the local school and was of German descent. Discipline was number one on the agenda. We were taught to march, learn the history of the German people, and participate in athletic sports with emphasis on winning competitions. Each youth was given a personal book, containing a list of various sport activities like swimming, gymnastics, running, bicycling, skiing, target shooting, wrestling, boxing, fencing, etc. to be tried and judged. For each event, a participant was given a score that was recorded and stamped off by the instructors. When the entire book was completed, a gold, silver, bronze, or black medal was awarded. Gold, of course, was the best and black was passing. I received a silver arrow, inscribed with the words, "Outstanding Sportsmanship and Perseverance." I must admit that being involved with sports was enjoyable and exciting. Soccer and ice hockey were my favorites.

Since I showed a desire to become an airplane pilot, I was given a chance to practice glider training for two years, attending classes that emphasized all aspects of flying from wind variables to balancing. Strapped in a seat of a small glider, attached to a rope and pulled by other team members, I managed to fly about one hundred feet above the ground for a short distance. I loved it and progressed to the next stage when a motor cable whizzed me about five hundred feet above the ground. Releasing the cable, I glided for about fifteen minutes. I was disappointed when I could not complete the final stages for gliding mastery because of supply shortages. This thrilling gliding experience is fresh in my memory until today.

As my final school year was coming to an end, I expressed interest in pursuing a career as a pilot. Shortly before graduation, Grandfather Fuchs suggested that he might be able to help with enrollment in Officers Flight School. He thought that his title as senator emeritus, along with my desire and experiences in gliding, might influence the directors of the school to accept me into the aviation program. Writing a letter, he received a reply that the classes were full and that I should apply for the next year's program. My dream of becoming a pilot was not to be fulfilled, even though I had intentions of applying to flight school the following year. Once a student finished school, the government dictated his or her job placement based on employment needs for the community or town of residency, so I was assigned to work as an electrician's apprentice because of the manpower shortage in this field. I was employed as an electrician for about six months, working for the city of Linz.

At the end of 1944, I was drafted into the *Arbeits Dinst*, which was a paramilitary work service. Instead of using rifles we used shovels. This unit was similar to the army engineers. We built roads, small bridges, reinforced embankments on the rivers caused by erosion, constructed barracks, and repaired buildings and roads.

In April of 1945, the American troops marched into northern Austria. The men in my work battalion and I were taken as prisoners of war. Luckily, the U.S. Army occupied Austria, and we were POWs for two weeks, the length of time it took to process and investigate backgrounds to conclude that we were noncombatants and no threat to the Americans. I was released approximately one hundred miles northeast of Linz, where my family resided. Since there was no means of transportation home, a buddy and I began our long walk back to Linz. Each of us received a loaf of bread, two cans of meat, and a canteen of water. As we walked, we decided to take short cuts through fields and forests along the countryside. Thankfully, I had a pocket compass that accurately directed us, but after a few days, we ran out of food. Attempting to stop at farms for food, the farmers were afraid to help strangers. We were desperate and decided to use the bottom cup of our canteens to boil water and grass to make soup. That was a mistake! Dreadful dysentery developed. Running out of cigarettes contributed more stress to our situation. Fortunately, one farmer took pity and gave us several boiled potatoes and sausages. It was a sumptuous meal, nourishing our bodies and improving our dispositions. Painful blisters had formed on our feet, but we continued walking. About ten miles from our destination, an American GI stopped his truck and gave us a most appreciated ride. Upon arriving in Linz, my buddy and I parted, heading in different directions.

My family rejoiced at my safe return, but the main topic of discussion at Camp Auhof, where my family resided, was the shocking news that a Nazi concentration camp existed only fifteen miles away. We had been told that the camp was a military facility, but it had been actually occupied by Russian and Ukrainian prisoners. Some of the survivors moved into our camp. A year later, my cousin Alexandria married Paul Kolodnicky, who was one of the survivors. Renee, my girlfriend, and I decided that we would also marry as soon as the situation improved.

Within a month's time, it was decided that Austria would be divided into four sectors, with one sector being maintained by the United States, one by Great Britain, one by France, and one by the Soviet Union. Vienna, the capital of Austria, was totally in the Russian zone. Vienna would also be divided into four sections, similar to Berlin. The Russians would rule Auhof, where we resided. I realized that Russian rule would mean dictatorship where individuals did not count and sublimation to the state would be enforced, and more frightening, all refugees and displaced persons would be transported immediately to Russia. It would be tragic for my family to remain in the Russian sector, especially because of Father's past history.

Upon hearing the frightful news of the Russian occupation, my parents and five-year-old brother, Alex, immediately packed their belongings and traveled over the Nibelungen Bridge crossing the Danube River to the American zone, relocating into military barracks abandoned by the Germans. One of these barracks became their new home. Each barrack consisted of four small rooms. My parents used two rooms and another family used the other two rooms. Grandfather Fuchs, his youngest daughter, Helena, and her family (husband, Eugene; daughter, Alexandria; and her fiancé, Paul) also moved to a barrack adjacent to my parents' barrack. Everyone tried to persuade me to accompany them, but I decided to stay at Camp Auhof with my fiancée and her family for a while.

Renee's family and my family were neighbors in the camp for years. At that time, I determined that Renee's mother, Anna, was an extremely unhappy woman. She was born in the part of Rumania that was controlled by the Austrian-Hungarian monarchy under the rule of Kaiser Franz Joseph. Anna's father was an Austrian general, who never married her mother. Anna's mother died a few years after Anna's birth, so her maternal grandmother raised her. Sadly, Anna never knew her father or her mother. Anna, an attractive woman, married Ladislaus, a handsome man, who owned two beauty salons in Bucharest, Rumania. They had three children: Lilly, Renee, and George.

Renee's family, like my family, was also transplanted to Austria because part of their heritage was German. There was little privacy in camp life. Everyone surmised that Renee's parents did not have a happy marriage. When Ladislaus was drafted into the German Army, Anna and her children were alone. She did not seem to convey love to them. In fact, she was excessively strict and abusive, especially to Renee, who was always instructed to help with all the chores. It was evident that no matter what Renee did, it never seemed to please her mother.

Verbal and physical abuse was inflicted upon Renee often. Was her mother jealous of her youth and beauty? I am not sure, but Renee did not deserve this brutal treatment. Anna rarely punished Lilly. Perhaps being two years older and more independent than Renee saved her. Lilly was off attending dance classes and theatrical performances, so she was not around. Little brother George was too young, so abuse was not inflicted on him, but poor Renee got the brunt of it. On one occasion, Anna came after Renee with a large spoon and was about to strike her, when I jumped between them and was struck instead. She had a mean swing! I tried to reason with Anna, but to no avail. All I could do was sympathize and comfort Renee. We had grown up together and had fallen in love.

Ladislaus served with the German forces as a medic throughout most of the war. Fighting on the Russian front, his unit eventually retreated to the southern part of Germany when the war ended. The German Army dissolved, and he walked home, arriving at Camp Auhof a few weeks after me. Loving his children and treating me like a son, Ladislaus was delighted that I would be his son-in-law, marrying his favorite daughter.

While we were in camp, a Rumanian delegation, consisting of two high-ranking officers, announced that anyone from Rumania could return and regain their properties. This offer was very attractive to Ladislaus and his family, since he felt there was no future staying in Austria. After discussing the possibility of my accompanying them to Rumania with the delegation officials, we learned that there would be no problem as long as I was part of the family, so I decided to go with them. Following the woman I loved was a happy decision.

After registering, we were told that in a month a train would be provided to transport all families choosing to relocate to Rumania. Meanwhile, the Russians occupied upper Austria, including our section. They closed the borders between the Russian and American sectors. Now, I was not permitted to visit my family or anyone else across the Danube River, the natural divider between the American and Russian districts. Feelings of anxiety caused mixed emotions. I questioned myself on whether I had made the right choice, yet I had no recourse but to follow through on my commitment.

Sitting around and waiting for a month was not in my plans. I needed to earn money, so I went to the employment office in search of a job. While I was there, I read a poster advertising a position as a Russian interpreter for the local government. I knew that I would qualify, so I applied for the position. After being interviewed, I was hired, soon discovering that I had been the only applicant. I was thankful to have a job in a small office in the municipal building in Urfahr, the seat of the local government for the Russian occupied zone. Prior to the occupation, Urfahr had been a section of Linz, Austria. Because Urfahr was no longer part of the city of Linz, the Russians were in complete control. The Russian military authorities had merely appointed Austrians as figureheads of the local governing body. Since Austrians did not speak Russian, it was my job to translate any orders and correspondences from the "true" governing Russians. Of course, I made no mention of the fact that in approximately a month I would be going to Rumania with my fiancée and her family.

For the next few weeks, I was busily translating all sorts of directives. One of the first orders was to the transportation department in reference to the Russian personnel using the public transportation vehicles like the trolleys and busses free of charge. Another directive mentioned that certain office buildings must be vacated for Russian military use only. During my third week of employment, a Russian colonel requested to meet "the translator." We met and naturally conversed in Russian. He inquired about my accurate articulation and knowledge of the Russian language. I told him the truth that I studied Russian in school, and the next question was "What school in Russia did you attend?"

I responded, "I was never in Russia. I learned the language in a private school in Poland." The colonel insisted that my pronunciation was too perfect to have been learned in a school setting in a foreign country and continued his probing questions. I did not dare to reveal that I spoke Russian at home and that my father was a former czarist officer. I had to show him my passport, which documented my birth in Vilnius (Wilno), Poland. I could tell he was still skeptical. He recorded everything I had said on his notepad. Then, before he departed, he commanded that I be in his office in two weeks, setting an appointment for an exact time and date. I knew he was planning to investigate my background thoroughly, and if we ever met again, I would surely be sent to Siberia. Thank God, within a few days, the train to Rumania arrived and I was on board.

On the day of departure, my anxious thoughts and concerns for the future intertwined with feelings of excitement and fear of the unknown, yet I soon settled down and focused on the basic objective, going to Rumania. A coal-driven locomotive pulled several passenger cars and two baggage cars that were located at the end of the train. We implicitly followed the orders of the Rumanian officers who informed us that our suitcases and other belongings must be placed in the baggage cars at the rear. Finally, we were on our way, yet my anxieties still surfaced, as we traveled through Austria toward Vienna, passing the Russian sector. The train stopped two times for inspection by the military, and each time the Rumanian officers would explain that the train was heading to Rumania with Rumanian citizens. Miraculously, the Russians never boarded the train to talk to the passengers.

The Wesbahnhof train station in Vienna, in the French occupied sector, was a transfer station where trains would be transferred onto different tracks to continue journeying east. As we arrived at the station, we were informed that our train would be parked overnight on one side of the track, and in the morning the train cars would be connected to continue on our way. We were strongly advised not to leave the cars. This request seemed reasonable since we were in the French zone and did not possess French credentials.

The next morning, we patiently waited and waited, but nothing happened. We shockingly discovered that the Rumanian officers and the two baggage cars were missing. Most of us were distraught, and some were hysterical, and others simply wept because deception by fellow human beings hurts. Whatever we had on our person was all we possessed. The post-war situation was chaotic and ruthless. It was a time when evil prevailed and greedy people surfaced, easily taking advantage of desperate people who wanted to find a place to live in peace. Feeling disheartened, I kept thinking about my one and only suit that was in my luggage. Some of us could not contemplate that we had been cruelly tricked and everything was really gone.

As a group, we approached the Austrian railroad authorities for answers with no satisfaction. It was a hopeless situation. The local police and the French authorities directed us to the Red Cross that was located outside the station. The volunteers at the Red Cross served soup and bread for lunch and suggested that we remain in the railroad cars until better shelters could be provided. Each of us was given a blanket and returned to the train cars.

After lengthy discussions and feelings of impatience, Renee's father, another refugee, and I decided not to stay in the train but to search the surrounding area for better accommodations. We decided to help ourselves. We discovered that the streets and part of the train station were damaged from the bombings during the war, yet an empty, large tool shack on the railroad property was still intact and would be a better accommodation than the train car.

The next morning, the three of us approached the stationmaster to ask about work, specifically cleaning out the bombed station. We also requested permission to stay in the tool shack. He agreed to both requests. We began working for meager wages. The Red Cross gave us pillows, old mattresses, and food. Creative ingenuity combined with hard labor turned the shed into a home for our two families. Large wooden cabinets were turned over and used as beds. It was better than sleeping on the floor. We converted the larger of the two rooms in the shack into sleeping areas for each family, dividing the room in half with old tent material that we found and hung from a line in the middle of the room. The smaller room contained a round, tin tub that we converted into a bathtub. Adjacent to the tub was a toilet without a seat. After our repairs, it flushed. There was a cold-water faucet, but no sink, so we constructed a sink out of a tin barrel, which probably was previously used for storing gasoline. We cut it in half, turned the top with the spout upside down and connected the spout to a drainage tube in the floor. The make shift bathroom sufficed our needs. A potbellied stove for heating and cooking was primitive, yet boiling water for a cup of tea was a luxury. We collected the empty food cans from the Red Cross, using the smallest cans for cups and largest cans for cooking. Whatever we found in the rubble, we used. We were becoming excellent recyclers, reusing everything.

Receiving an assortment of clothing from the Red Cross was beneficial. This organization provided us with all sorts of things since there were limited items available in the few stores that were opened. We did not have enough money for the "black market" where you could obtain almost anything for the right price. Was my one good suit in the black market or did it travel to Rumania or all the way to Russia?

All of us were consumed with working hard every minute of every day to improve our living conditions, but after a few weeks, the effects of overworking and under eating caused me to become sick. Running a high fever was one symptom, followed a few days later with my skin turning yellow. Even my eyeballs and nails were yellow. I spent three weeks in the local hospital and the diagnosis was yellow jaundice, most likely caused from malnutrition. The menu they served me was limited to a special diet including a glass of *Karlsbader Salt* mixed with water for breakfast and a bowl of soup made from a potato puree mixed with water for lunch. It tasted awful! I was given a 20cc injection of a grape sugar mixture and various medications. At last, my normal color returned, and I was sent home.

My protruding ribs made me appear very thin, yet amazingly my weight was recorded as one hundred twenty-five pounds. The doctors concluded that my bones were healthy, heavy, and strong, and good health would return. I was thankful that during my youth, Mother had fed me nourishing meals and followed the advice of our family physician, Dr. Rosenberg, to feed me chicken, milk, and lots of vegetables as often as possible. Their combined teamwork to produce a strong boy seemed to have worked!

My body fully recuperated, but my mind was troubled and in turmoil. After a month, I realized that I could no longer continue living a life of drudgery with no hope for a future, no hope of seeing my family again, since I could not cross the Russian occupied zone, and absolutely no hope of marrying and starting my own family. I did not want to subject my children to such poverty and uncertainty. Extremely depressed, I longed to find a way out of my despairing life.

French Foreign Legion

My quest for a new life was answered unexpectedly on a peaceful Sunday. As I walked through the park listening to the French military band, I stopped to read a recruiting poster for the French Foreign Legion. It displayed a picture of a legionnaire and stated specific promises of a better life with the particular enticement of acquiring French citizenship after five years of service. Since I was a displaced person with no country, joining the French Foreign Legion would finally give me the opportunity to be identified with a country and begin a new life. My prayers had been answered.

The next day I arrived at the French Army's headquarters of the Jura Alpine Battalion to inquire about joining the Legion. The French Army Battalion in Vienna occupied an old military fortress that was constructed before World War I and was used by the Germans during World War II. A huge enclosed complex, the fortress housed the soldiers comfortably. The officer in charge explained that he had no official registration forms for the legionnaires, but I could sign a letter of intent to join for five years. Concurring with me that my life would be better off than it was now, the officer mentioned that the only way for me to cross the Russian zone into France was to stay with his unit and be included as part of the regular French military transport that would be leaving in two weeks. When the unit stopped over in Strasbourg, France, I would be turned over to the authorities in the French Foreign Legion. He also suggested that I go to the local police department to obtain an affidavit that I was not a criminal or running away from the law. I agreed to everything and was given a special pass that would admit me to the military post upon my return. Thanking him for the information, I left, committed in my goal to join the French Foreign Legion. I would become a French citizen and be able to go any place in the world after my discharge. It was a choice of hope for the future, especially for a young man who just turned eighteen years old.

Explaining my final and firm decision to join the French Foreign Legion to Renee and her family was not easy, but they also realized that staying in the present situation was misery and that I needed to do something positive, moving my life forward. Staying in Austria was a hopeless existence, because I was not an Austrian citizen and declared a displaced person without a country. It was difficult to leave, yet I knew I could not sit around and wait.

Upon returning to the French Army's post, I was assigned a cot in the barrack and given work clothes for a job as a helper in the kitchen until the regiment left for France. I was also told about my important job to make coffee and to have it ready by six o'clock each morning. The wood-fueled stove was a mobile unit that could be hooked to a truck for transport to different areas. The stove rested on a trailer with two large rubber wheels and accommodated a fifty-gallon-sized kettle that served as a huge coffee pot. Parked next to the stove was another trailer loaded with wooden logs. The facility used as a kitchen was adjacent to the mobile unit.

Awaking at five o'clock in the morning on my very first day at the military post, I proceeded to fulfill my obligation of making the coffee, but I encountered difficulty igniting a flame because the firewood was too moist. I had the bright idea of pouring gasoline over the wood. Once I threw the match onto the gasoline soaked wood, a loud explosion erupted, but a good fire was started. When the cooks in the kitchen heard the blast, they ran outside to find out what had happened, and soon determined it was just my method to light the fire that caused the noise. Though I did not fully understand what the cooks were saying, their gestures and laughter conveyed that they thought the incident was funny, and from then on, whenever they heard a blast, they knew that I was making coffee. Until the day when making the coffee was not a laughing matter because I carelessly poured gasoline, not only on the wood, but also on the tire that started to burn. I frantically ran into the kitchen, grabbed the fire extinguisher to douse the flames on the tire. I still managed to have the coffee ready on time. From then on, I was meticulously careful about lighting the fire.

Granted permission to leave the post with packages of leftover food that I would give to Renee and her family made me feel good to be helping them and eased my sorrow about leaving. I would visit as often as I could, and they were thankful for every morsel of food, and I was grateful for their loving encouragement.

The day I packed my belongings and boarded the train departing for France, Renee and everyone in her family arrived at the station to wish me good luck and a safe trip. Renee and I cried, yet realized that clinging to one another was not the answer. We promised to write. I vowed to return after my tour of duty. Waving hands were the last things I saw as the train chugged away. Stopping at the Russian occupied check point in Vienna was a tense time for me, but fortunately the French commanding officer was the only one who left the train to speak to the Russian officer in charge, showing him official documents that all aboard were French soldiers. I was truly on my way to a new life.

Stopping for about fifteen minutes in Linz, Austria, where my parents resided in the American zone, was one of the most agonizing minutes of my life. I had known since the beginning that the designated train route would pass through Linz, but I was surprised that the train had stopped. I silently debated the pros and cons on whether to leave the train and go home to my parents or stay on the train and continue my commitment to be a legionnaire. There was a struggle within my mind and soul for my actions must now truly be committed to the words I professed. I realized that my decision would be a turning point in my life. Not moving from my seat, I gazed out the window, continuing my internal debate with the realization that I could justifiably abandon my plans since I had simply signed a paper of intent to join the Legion and it was not a valid document. I had not been officially sworn in and did not take an oath to stay, thus concluding that I could walk away, but then I reasoned that staying with the soldiers was a chance for a better life, with adventures and exciting opportunities. Fond memories, from when I was age ten viewing movies glamorizing the heroic life of legionnaires battling in the African desert, surfaced. I recalled telling my father, "I want to join the French Foreign Legion." He would laugh and say that when you grow up there will be other things to do. My childhood fantasy could become a reality. The Legion was a challenging path to follow, an interesting life to experience, and a destiny to fulfill. It would be my choice. Free will is a wonderful freedom as long as those making the choices can abide by the course of actions morally and honorably. I stayed on the train.

The third stop was Salzburg, and the last stop in Austria was Innsbruck in the French occupied zone. At the final destination, Strasbourg, France, the soldiers and I disembarked, and then I was transferred to a detachment of legionnaires. Their headquarters was a staging center for new recruits. About two hundred men of various nationalities were registering along with me, but the majority of the enlistees were former German soldiers. Passports were collected and work uniforms were issued. Everyone was subjected to a preliminary medical examination and assigned to a barrack and some sort of work detail. I once again was assigned to chores in the kitchen. After an oral interview, I answered lots of questions on several forms that were written in my native language. Then I signed a contract promising to complete five years of service in the French Foreign Legion. A new photograph was taken and included in my personal file. Everyone accepted as a legionnaire was placed on probationary period for six months.

Once preliminary registrations were completed, the other recruits and I were transported to Fort St. Nicholas in Marseille, in the southern part of France, where further processing occurred, including more detailed medical examinations and security checks with Interpol. I was a part of a group of thirty men in a section that was similar to a platoon of soldiers in the U.S. Army. A corporal, our immediate instructor, was in charge. In the Legion the rank of a corporal is equivalent to a sergeant in the U.S. Army, and his commands must be respected and unequivocally obeyed.

The next requirement for all recruits was the shaving of our heads. Then one by one, we stripped down to our underwear. Our belongings were catalogued and put in a duffel bag for storage (never to be seen again). We were allowed to keep our toiletries. I finally felt the joy of being a legionnaire, when my permanent uniform was issued, and I began singing and marching with the troops, but my elation did not last. The daily routine of rising at five o'clock each morning, exercising, attending classes, adhering to all sorts of rules and regulations, completing various work details and other laborious tasks, like hand-washing my uniform and hanging it up to dry, and cleaning the barracks, was exhausting and tedious. One difficult rule was that no one was permitted to communicate with the outside world. I was not living the glamorous life of a legionnaire as I had expected.

Ordered to speak French exclusively, all recruits attended classes daily to learn the language. The instructor used the see-and-say method. Pointing to an object, he would pronounce its name in French, and we would repeat the word after him. The first words I mastered was *kepi blanc*, referring to the legionnaire's famous white hat. Eventually this boring see-and-say method helped me to communicate in French and to improve my basic needs. Some legionnaires were fluent in French and were paired with a non-French-speaking partner. My partner helped me to interpret specific commands that I would not have been able to follow without his assistance.

Gradually, I adjusted to the military setting at Fort St. Nicholas, where I was stationed for several weeks. Located at the entrance of fishermen's harbor at the top of a hill, Fort St. Nicholas was a huge fortress surrounded by an outside wall approximately fifty feet high. The inside part of the wall housed the living quarters for the legionnaires and the other military facilities. There was a huge courtyard in the center where the French flag and the Legion's banner were proudly displayed at the top of tall poles. The top perimeter of the fortress consisted of walkways ten feet wide, where centuries before, cannons stood to protect the harbor from invaders. Each recruit was assigned guard duty, to walk solely around the perimeter of the wall. On clear days, guard duty was a delight because of the magnificent view of the harbor and the fishermen unloading their catch. They would feast on clams, French bread, and bottles of wine. Strictly forbidden to leave the fort at anytime, my view was limited to tranquil scenes of the simple life of the fishermen. While observing their easygoing lifestyle, I began to wonder whether I had made the right choice of joining the Legion. Before I could ponder too long over my concerns, I was boarding a British destroyer and off to my next destination, Oran, Algeria.

Once aboard the destroyer, another new legionnaire and I volunteered to help the British kitchen crew and were assigned to my least favorite job of washing pots and pans, but the cooks treated us well. Communicating by signs and gestures because of our language barrier, the good-natured cooks would pat our bald heads indicating approval of our work. My fellow volunteer and I also had access to extra food and cigarettes, benefits that were most appreciated.

During the crossing of the Mediterranean Sea on two occasions, we heard the loud blasts from the ship's cannons. Later we learned that the cannons were targeting German mines that were floating in the water. Thankfully, all the mines were destroyed before damaging the vessel.

As the destroyer traveled closer to North Africa, the air temperature escalated and breathing became more difficult, especially after disembarking. I felt like a fish out of water, at times gasping for air. All the new legionnaires were quickly hustled into a military infirmary located at the Oran harbor. Each one of us was given an injection between the shoulder blades, ordered to rest on a cot, and warned not to eat or drink anything for twenty-four hours. If we disobeyed, we would become violently ill. One man ate something and became sick. He was moved to another area. His violation of the rules enforced obedience from all the others. The following day, we were miraculously able to breathe normally and withstand the excruciatingly hot climate. In fact, I rarely perspired much ever again or was bothered by extremely hot weather, yet before receiving the injection, I would perspire in the wintertime. Until today, I have no idea of what type of medication was used to alleviate our heat problems. Whatever the substance, it quickly readied us to be transported by train to Sidi-Bel-Abbes, West Algeria, near Spanish Morocco, the largest French Foreign Legion depot. This facility was the central headquarters for the training and deployment of legionnaire troops.

My barrack was across the street from the famous French Foreign Legion military band, Musique Principale. Once a year for Bastille Day, the band would travel to Paris and lead the parade, commemorating the destruction of the Bastille, a state prison in Paris, during the French Revolution. In Sidi-Bel-Abbes, the band practiced every day, marching ten abreast. When they marched down the boulevard, all the windows rattled. Their performance was most impressive! I especially liked seeing the drums being carried at the lower ring at knee level and the horns adorned with the Legion flag that would be twirled around in a salute after the completion of a song. I would watch them as often as I could, wishing that I were more musically inclined to become a member of the band.

The most unique memorial, dedicated to the heroism of the legionnaires, was erected in the middle of the complex at Sidi-Bel-Abbes. It was a huge-bronze globe, inscribed with the names of every country where legionnaires fought and with the motto, "*Legio Patria Nostra*," when translated means "The Legion is our fatherland." Four life-size sculptures of legionnaires surrounded the globe, and each statue represented a legionnaire dressed in a uniform from a different era, beginning with the Legion's origin in 1813 to World War II. In 1970 this monument was transported to Aubagne, France, the present recruiting center for legionnaires.

In my section or platoon, I was one of about thirty men from all over the world. To encourage more unity, heterogeneous groups were emphasized to promote loyalty only to the Legion rather than to one's native country. It was stictly prohibited to refer to anyone by his nationality. We were all legionnaires united with the words, "one for all and all for one," yet we were all foreigners who could not understand one another to carry on friendly conversations. Communicating in French was difficult, for most of the vocabulary we had learned pertained to military equipment, commands, and drills. The majority of us could not speak socially, as buddies would talk to one another. It was depressing in the beginning, because my life was a lonely existence. I soon realized that camaraderie and friendship were as important as obedience, loyalty, bravery, and honor. Even though daily duties were completed with solidarity, tradition, and teamwork, at times it was strange not confiding in another human about personal feelings. Needing to discuss or share ideas with a fellow human is important. When it was reported that two men from my section had deserted, I could understand their desperation. Rumors surfaced that they had been caught before they reached the border of Morocco, but I was never sure what happened to them.

Basic training was rough and tough, with hours and hours of strenuous physical exercise, singing and marching, and training with weapons for desert combat. Discipline was implicitly emphasized and drilled continuously. Being in control of every action no matter what the circumstances was practiced and perfected. If a legionnaire was at attention and a mosquito landed on his face, he would not be permitted to swat it off or even blink or twitch. Punishment was severe, consisting of completing numbers of push-ups, non-stop running, or hours of marching. Showing respect to all officers was demanded, otherwise physical punishment like a slap or a punch would be inflicted. Major disobedience could lead to a court-martial or jail time, but usually the jail time was suspended and additional service time extended the unconditional, five-year contract.

During early morning revelry, the corporal always kicked the last legionnaire out of the barrack, so I tried never to be the last man out. On occasion, the corporal would quietly approach a legionnaire sleeping in his bunk and stand and stare. If there were no signs or reactions from the sleeping legionnaire, the corporal would strike his nose with the flick of two fingers, causing a painful and rude awakening. The purpose of his actions was to teach alertness at all times. Basic training seemed like sixteen weeks in hell.

Legionnaires cannot be fussy eaters. Breakfast consisted of strong, black coffee, a can of sardines, and crackers. For lunch, lots of vegetables, mostly carrots, peas, artichokes, and dates, along with a canteen filled with wine were served. Since my previous experience with wine consisted of merely sampling Grandfather Fuchs' homemade brew, I was not accustomed to drinking wine everyday. I felt tipsy at first, but later I became used to the daily consumption of alcohol. Sometimes at dinner, a lamb stew or a delicacy of donkey meat that was cooked in wine was served. Donkey meat was tender and delicious, but it took a while for me to try it. Potatoes were rarely served. Rice and noodles were plentiful. Dates and figs were always available. Though the meals served were not my favorites, they were excellent compared to having no food during the war. At least I was never hungry, and my body grew stronger.

After sixteen weeks of training, a ceremony was held to present each recruit with a cap that was blue rimmed with a red top, upon which was fastened a white cover. Replacing the woolen khaki bonnet, previously worn, I could officially wear the legionnaire's *kepi blanc*. A major requirement was to keep the white cover spotless. I would wash the white cover often and pull it over the *kepi*. The cover would dry within minutes.

Appointed to Company Number 3, Third Regiment, my fellow legionnaires and I were assigned guard duty at the base or more dangerous patrols in the desert for as long as a week. We would capture Algerian rebels committing crimes against the French and confiscate contraband of war. The rebels wanted their independence and hated the French, causing the legionnaires to become their prime targets.

When stationed on the home base on weekends, passes were distributed to go into the town of Sidi-Bel-Abbes with one stipulation: do not go into the Coz Bah (casbah), an area where unsavory characters congregated. Most of the legionnaires heeded the warning that the Coz Bah was off limits, but unfortunately some legionnaires were lured into the Coz Bah with promises of sexual favors from prostitutes and were knifed to death. Vivid in my memory is May 1, 1946, the dreadful day that the legionnaires were killed. From that day on, no one was allowed to venture to town alone without weapons.

After numerous patrol missions, I observed that the Algerian rebels were ruthless and cunning, causing all legionnaires to be alert and on guard at all times. I understood why the corporal flicked our noses to test awareness of our surroundings while we slept. Survival tactics practiced were used and appreciated when involved in combat. Before we were sent to a combat area, sometimes a ration of cognac, instead of wine, was distributed. At first, I thought it was most generous to be drinking the more expensive liquor, but later I realized that the cognac became a stimulant for courage to fight, especially when outnumbered. At the canteen wine was cheaper than a bottle of pure well water. Water cost twelve francs compared to red wine that sold for only nine francs, another factor contributing to its popularity.

On my last patrol heading west of Sidi-Bel-Abbes toward Morocco into the Atlas Mountains, my company of legionnaires was in a bivouac overnight. While sleeping, the Algerian rebels ambushed us, but we succeeded in driving them away, however during the fight, I was wounded. Slashed by a sword on my left, upper leg, the wound bled profusely. The medic cleaned and bandaged the seven-inch gash, but upon returning to the base, my leg was infected causing a high fever. I was transported to the hospital in Oran and was unconscious for several days. I briefly awoke and was told that I was being carried by stretcher onto a British airplane carrier, leaving for France.

The next time I awoke, I was in a colonial army hospital in Toulon, in the south of France, where a doctor explained the happenings of the past few weeks and the serious fact that my leg was almost amputated. Another surprise was that all my belongings were gone, including my complete uniform and a valuable souvenir dagger. I was shockingly upset, confused, and angry. With the aid of crutches, I hobbled to the hospital administrative office determined to obtain a more detailed explanation from someone in authority. I did not consider the fact that the skimpy hospital gown exposing my naked buttocks was not suitable attire for a stroll in the hallway. Seeing a staff officer behind the desk, I began complaining in my "best French." Being agitated, I forgot the word for stolen, so the reasons for my anger were not understood. To make matters worse, I heard laughter and giggles behind me. Turning around, I saw two ladies smiling and pointing at me. Even though my face glowed scarlet red from embarrassment, I quickly covered myself the best I could and continued to express my complaints until I was completely understood. After a while a new legionnaire's uniform was sent to me, but my other personal possessions were gone forever.

I spent a few more weeks in the hospital with excellent medical care, yet I was still unable to walk without the use of crutches. Each morning, a staff of doctors would make rounds to visit patients checking on their progress. On one of the daily visits, the chief surgeon accompanied the regular group of physicians. Stopping to talk to me, he amicably inquired about my nationality and birthplace. When I responded that I was born in Vilnius (Wilno), the surgeon smiled and stated, "I was born there, too." He invited me to stop by his office later on to reminisce about our home in Vilnius (Wilno). I readily agreed and arrived at his office in the afternoon. Since he was of Polish descent, and Polish was easier for me to speak than French, we conversed comfortably in Polish. We chatted about the city and the people, and I talked at length about the events in my life. After revealing my personal history, he asked me an interesting question, "Do you want to leave the French Foreign Legion?"

I told him that I had signed a contract to stay in the Legion for five years and that I had about three and a half more years to serve before I could leave. The surgeon repeated, "I did not ask you if you could leave? I asked if you wanted to leave."

Bewildered, I slowly answered, "Yes, I would like to leave and return to my family, but how could that be possible?"

The confident surgeon said, "Leave it up to me."

Returning to my room with feelings of hope and the possibility of another change in my life, I realized that everyone's future was filled with uncertainties. Life was like walking through a maze with twists and turns and dead-ends. Father's words echoed in my mind, "Be optimistic in life. When you have tried your best to remedy any predicament, place your fate in God's hands for you are no longer in control." I agreed with Father and instead of festering over the matter, I decided to concentrate on recuperating and prayed that God would look favorably on my destiny.

Retuning to the hospital ward that accommodated me and about a dozen other patients, I sat on my bed and nodded hello to Pierre whose bed was next to mine. Pierre, a Frenchman who was also recovering from combat injuries, was about thirty years old and a sergeant in one of the French colonial regiments stationed originally in West Africa. He had befriended me and took on the role of an older brother. Even with my limited French vocabulary, we conversed as much as possible, for Pierre was a pleasant, fun-loving individual.

Familiar with the city of Toulon, he convinced me to take a break from the hospital environment and join him to see the sites. We boarded a streetcar and rode a couple of miles into a section of town where the houses appeared deserted. After disembarking, I followed him into one of the houses, and as soon as the door opened, music and smoke poured out. The building must have been sound-proof because the noise surprised me. We entered a room that was a tavern with round tables and chairs and a long bar with stools. Girls greeted us. We had a good time. My first and only experience in the red light district in Toulon with an attractive, professional prostitute who was about twenty years old was a complete surprise and the sergeant's treat. He paid for everything. The hours passed by quickly, and on the ride back to the hospital, the sergeant and I agreed that humans desire intimacy. As a steady customer, Pierre's desires were definitely being fulfilled.

Using a cane instead of crutches was an indication that my leg was getting stronger. I was happy to be healing, but my spirits really soared when the chief surgeon read an official document announcing my medical discharge from the Legion. His words were unbelievable. My career in the French Foreign Legion was over, with no chance of obtaining French citizenship. I wondered if I would ever find a country.

Shortly after the news of my medical discharge, reports arrived explaining that my entire regiment was nearly wiped out in Indochina (Vietnam). If I had not been injured and had remained with my section of legionnaires, most likely I would have been one of the casualties. Returning to the status of a displaced person with no country seemed like a minor predicament compared to the devastating consequences that could have occurred in my life. Once again, I considered myself very fortunate.

Events in my life happened quickly. Within the next two days, I received transportation papers and a ticket to Paris. Reporting to the Legion's military offices, I exchanged my uniform for civilian clothes and was given the remainder of my salary. Issued a new passport and a train ticket, I was on my way to Linz, Austria.

The fact that I cannot remember the chief surgeon's name, no matter how hard I think, truly bothers me, for he is an important person and responsible for affecting my life. Why did he help me? Did I touch his heart about my sad story? Did fond memories of friends and family surface after conversations about Vilnius (Wilno)? Did he want to be a father figure and assist a young man on a conflicting crossroad? Whatever his reason, his name may be forgotten, but his benevolent deed, that permitted me to return to my family and begin a new life once again, will live with me forever.

Linz, Austria

Linz, the town of my youth, greeted me with comforting surroundings and feelings of joy. I rode the streetcar half way across town toward the Danube River, bringing me closer to home. As I gazed through the window of the slowly moving trolley, I reflected over my experiences of the past two years, including the people I encountered, the decisions made by me and for me, and the progression of simply growing up. No longer a boy, but now a man, I had matured in mind as well as body. My physical appearance was different. My blond hair, bleached by the sun, and my skin, dark and tan in color, revealed a new me. In fact, I stood out among the fair-skinned Austrians, whose stares made me feel self-conscious, yet it did not matter for I was thrilled to be in the city I loved.

Exiting the streetcar and still using a cane, I walked slowly through the familiar streets onto Obere Donaulande near the *tabak fabrik*, the tobacco factory, across the street from my parent's residence. Since the last communication sent to them was from Sidi-bel-Abbes, Algeria, I realized my arrival would be an amazing shock. Anxiously quickening my pace, I finally approached the barrack and saw Father standing outside near the vegetable garden. I called out, "Pop, it's me." Turning to look, he did not recognize me at first, but then he ran into my arms hugging me tightly.

Mother, peering through the window, told me later that she could not understand why Father was embracing a stranger, but as soon as I spoke, she knew it was me and ran out squealing with joy with seven-year-old Alex following right behind.

Mother's nurturing ways never seemed to change. Catering to my every whim and concerned about my injury, I was pampered daily. Both my leg and my spirit grew stronger. Being home was the best medicine. It was fun reacquainting myself to family life. For several days I explained the happenings of every aspect of the past two years to my parents and Alex, who would sit next to me listening carefully to every word. They in turn would share the latest news about their life in Linz that was also changing for the better. Father was now working in the maintenance department for the 124th United States Army General Hospital, a few blocks away on Lederergasse Street.

When I no longer needed to walk with the use of a cane and was completely rested, Father suggested that I should apply for a job at the hospital where he was employed. I thought it was an excellent idea. Originally the Austrian hospital was a specialized maternity facility, but the American occupational forces transformed it into an army hospital with many Austrian workers employed in their previous positions. Father accompanied me to the office of the American personnel administrator who interviewed me in fluent German and asked me to fill out an application. Stressing my qualifications as an electrician, I was hired as an electrician's assistant by the United States Forces in Austria (USFA) and immediately assigned to work with George Musil, an electrical engineer, who was an Austrian. During the war, he had served in the German Navy as an engineer, and when the war ended, he returned to Linz and was hired by the Austrian hospital administrators. Our personalities were congenial, so we not only worked well together but also became best friends. George was a master instructor, teaching me well. I absorbed his skillful knowledge enabling me to complete my job expertly. Two other electricians were also on our team. It was 1947.

The electricity in Europe consisted of 220 volts or 380 volts with fifty cycles. Since all the American medical equipment was built for 120 volts and 60 cycles, the hospital in-house power was not compatible; therefore portable generators were needed to run the American equipment. The four 100-kilowatt generators and the two 60-kilowatt generators were housed inside a shed on the far edge of the hospital property. It was the electricians' responsibility to keep them operating on a twenty-four hour basis. I became a proficient worker in charge of running the diesel-fueled generators. Overseeing four men, we rotated shifts, assuring the hospital of continued power supply.

Extra assignments like installing X-ray machines, operating tables, and fixtures were completed skillfully and competently. Other duties included being on call to correct any other electrical problems throughout the hospital. With two different electrical systems, the jobs were more complicated and resulted in longer working time. For example, according to the European electrical code, all the wiring must be in a metal tube, enclosed inside a wall. Chiseling the stone and concrete walls to repair, replace, or add electricity was required, followed with patching the broken area as an additional workload.

Since we spent many hours on our job, at times as many as fifty to sixty hours a week, George Musil and I were given a rent-free apartment in a building occupied by enlisted men and American military personnel. It was across the street from the hospital on Gruber Strasse. We shared a spacious two-bedroom apartment, with a full kitchen, bathroom, and living room. Next-door to our apartment building was another building housing officers, doctors, nurses, and other American personnel. A direct telephone line from the hospital switchboard to our apartment phone was installed, in order for us to respond to any electrical emergencies, of which there were many. Our excellent work ethics and dedicated service were not only appreciated, but also rewarded. The hospital commanding officer, Colonel Dean, provided us with special privileges like eating in the dining room with the medical personnel and supplying army fatigues and shoes as part of a work uniform.

On our days off, George and I made time for fun. George's family lived outside of Vienna with one uncle residing in Linz. Uncle Musil was a wealthy and prominent lawyer who purchased seasonal passes for boxed seats at the Linz Opera House, also called the Landes Theater. Thanks to Uncle Musil, George and I became opera enthusiasts attending numerous performances. In fact, my daughter Carmen was named after one of my favorite operas.

On occasion, George would visit his sister and her family who lived in lower Austria called Burgenland. George's family would invite me to come along, but I could not because I was not an Austrian citizen and the Russians occupied that section. His sister was married to the owner of a winery, who would give George a five-gallon jug of a special wine that was made exclusively for family consumption. He would share this outstanding wine with me. The wine was slightly bubbly like champagne and tasted smooth and refreshing. No matter how much we drank, we never had hangovers. Instead on the next day, I would awake feeling warm and contented.

Since Austria's climate is conducive to participating in winter sports, George and I would choose to ski as often as possible, spending weekends at an Alpine mountain retreat. Skiing was a way to exercise, release tension, sightsee, meet and party with other skiers, and enjoy the breathtakingly beautiful landscapes in the Austrian Alps. Since most of the time my work duties were indoors, I especially enjoyed being outside in the fresh air.

On one occasion with the full moon aglow, lighting the snow-covered slopes, making it look almost like daylight, George and I decided to night ski. We were familiar with the ski slopes on the terrain, adding to our confidence; however we encountered difficulty judging the distance between the trees and us. Their shadows gave us a false perception of the location of the actual trees, causing us to ski too close to them. Nearing the end of the run, I misjudged my spatial relationship to one of the trees and crashed into it. The force of the crash hit my right ski and right shoulder, and twisted my body around the tree, breaking the wooden ski, and spraining my ankle. Fortunately, George was nearby and able to help me to the first aid station. In severe pain, my ankle was bandaged, and my body and ego were badly bruised. I did not ski for several months and vowed never to night ski again.

George and I had established a sincere friendship, respecting one another's achievements. To me, George was a genius in any electrical matters. Building a radio from scratch, he was able to receive frequencies from almost any part of the world. He was not only an expert in his field, but also a passionate teacher wanting to share his knowledge with others who showed interest. Whenever I asked him a question about electronics, his explanations were lengthy involving specifics about the smallest details. I soon learned to avoid asking him too many questions, particularly when I was busy or had another appointment.

The last time I saw George was in 1975. He was working for the Austrian government, in charge of locating individuals operating unlicensed radio stations, and he was married and the father of two sons and a daughter. Visiting his beautiful home in Linz on a mountainside that included a wine cellar tunneled into the mountain is one of my fondest memories of our times together. His brother-in-law was still supplying the best wines, and we sat for many hours sampling various wines and reminiscing about our youthful escapades in Linz. George Musil passed away in 1985 from a malignant brain tumor. He was a good friend, an outstanding scholar, and a fine gentleman who will always remain a positive influence in my life.

In the summer of 1949, Sergeant John Drushall, a six-foot-four Texan who had served in the First Calvary Division during World War II and was now in command of hospital security, befriended me. Speaking English well enough to converse intelligently, I talked often with the sergeant. We not only discussed business about the hospital, but also amicably talked about daily events, personal interests, and past experiences. He was especially impressed that I spoke multi-languages. During one of our chats the sergeant asked, "Would you be interested in working with me aboard the *Passau*, an excursion ship for the military personnel?"

"I am definitely interested," was my quick reply. I doubted that I would be granted a leave of absence to accept this new position for the summer, but surprisingly I was given permission from headquarters to serve with Sergeant Drushall aboard the ship.

The *Passau* was a passenger ship leased from the Austrian government by the American military for recreational purposes. It had side-driven paddles and a huge diesel engine. Since none of the ship's crew spoke English, including the captain, I was to be the interpreter and Sergeant Drushall's assistant manager. The sergeant coordinated his managerial duties with Lieutenant LaMattola, who was affiliated with the United Service Organizations (USO), in charge of public relations for the troops and instrumental in obtaining the *Passau* for trips on the Danube River. The lieutenant was also responsible for setting a schedule of cruise excursions. During the week, evening cruises lasting for about four hours were arranged, with two days designated for enlisted men and two days for officers. Each group alternated schedules on the weekends.

Accommodations on board the *Passau* were luxurious. At the front of the ship on the main deck, there was a large room that could seat about one hundred fifty people and that was similar to a cabaret with smaller tables and a stage used by the performers. On the stern side of the main deck, a dining room was large enough to seat about one hundred people and included an area with a dance floor and a section for a band. In the middle of the ship on the starboard side of the main deck were five cabins; one for the captain, another for the first mate, the third for Sergeant Drushall, one for me, and the last cabin was used as a dressing room for the entertainers. The engineer's cabin, a full service bar, and the kitchen were also in the middle of the ship, but on the port side. Below the main deck was the engine room and storage rooms for supplies. The *Passau* had an open top deck with benches, and above that deck was the pilot's wheelhouse with the smoke stack directly behind.

For the rest of the summer, the captain, the first mate, the sergeant, and I resided comfortably on the *Passau*. The kitchen staff and four members of the crew lived in a building next to the pier. Several waiters and cleaning staff arrived daily to ready the ship for passengers.

In addition to my duty as a translator, I was required to complete work schedules for the civilian personnel and to maintain the audio-equipment room, which included a public address system, microphones, and record players. The Red Cross provided many popular albums that I played during the week when the live performers were not available. Music by Glenn Miller, Harry James, Benny Goodman, Spike Jones, and various western musicians were special requests by everyone and played over and over again. These talented artists and their wonderful tunes are still my very favorite dancing and listening music. Working on board the *Passau* was more like a vacation than job.

During the week, the round trip on the Danube River was about four hours. Passengers would board about seven o'clock at night enjoying a fun-filled evening. The weekend trips were twice as long, starting at nine in the morning and cruising all the way to the German border and returning around six o'clock in the evening. A party atmosphere prevailed with lots of dancing, drinking, smoking, and laughing.

The middle of the Danube River was a neutral area since the river was the dividing border between the American and the Russian zones. Whenever we cruised, I controlled the outside speakers, turning them towards the Russian side and increasing the volume. I would watch the Russian guards seriously spying at us through their binoculars. One of my favorite Glenn Miller instrumentals, "American Patrol," and other popular tunes were played often and blared in the direction facing the Russians. Smiling pleasurably, I would notice the curious, yet agitated expressions on their faces. I enjoyed causing a bit of a disturbance for them, yet at the same time was relieved to be with the Americans and not subjected to the oppressions of the Communist Russians. I counted my blessings to be on the side of freedom.

The Saturday before the cruise ended, the *Passau* departed as usual, but it was raining and the weather continued to worsen, unexpectedly, as we puttered up stream. By the time the ship turned around to head back, the downpour was torrential! The river rose higher and higher. On the down stream approach to Linz, the captain became concerned that the ship would not be able to clear the Nibelungen Bridge and safely reach the dock that was about a quarter of a mile away on the other side of the bridge.

The captain ordered all passengers and crew to the main deck to secure positions. Traveling in the middle of the river, he steered the ship underneath the highest point of the bridge and switched the engines to a reverse motion. The current of the water was extremely powerful, and no matter what precautions the captain executed, the roof of the pilothouse and the smoke stack sheared off when the bridge was hit.

As soon as the engine conked out, control of the ship was completely lost, causing it to drift downstream past the bridge and the docking port. Trying to restart the engine was unsuccessful. Throwing anchors over the side, slowed the ship, but it still continued drifting around a bend, heading toward the Russian shoreline. Expecting the worst situation, a dangerous crash thankfully did not happen for the bottom of the ship simply screeched into the soft mud of the shoreline without too much damage. Using the public announcement system, Sergeant Drushall confidently assured us that there was no immediate danger of sinking and that help was on the way.

Even though the *Passau* was not equipped with ship-to-shore radio communications, we were close enough to see the commotion on the American side. Since the military vehicles were heading toward the river, the officials were aware that the *Passau* was stranded in the Russian zone. They quickly dispatched a motorboat to our ship to investigate.

After evaluating the situation, it was decided to commandeer all available boats to rescue the passengers and return them to the American zone before the Russians responded. It was too late. About twenty Russian soldiers arrived and were trying to figure out how to board the *Passau*. Sergeant Drushall ran to his cabin, returning with his Colt .45 pistol. He told me to follow him. As we stood on the bow of the main deck, which was jammed into the shore, he ordered me to tell the Russians, "This ship is an American property, and the first Russian who tries to board it, gets a bullet between his eyes." Though I was nervous, I translated loudly and clearly in fluent Russian. Stunned by the perfectly pronounced Russian words and the sight of the big Texan pointing the gun in their direction, the baffled Russians did not speak and made no attempt to board the *Passau*. Minutes ticked by slowly. It seemed like an eternity to me, but finally the rescue boats arrived to transport passengers to the American side. The captain and the crew remained aboard until the tugboats pulled the *Passau* into the shipyard for repairs. Just before the tugboats arrived, the sergeant and I were the last passengers to leave. From then on, all military cruise excursions on the Danube were canceled!

The sergeant and I returned to our jobs at the hospital, where the *Passau* incident was the prime topic of conversation for several days. We joked and laughed about the reactions from the Russians, but also admitted that the situation could have been more serious if the ship had been badly damaged. For me, it was an unforgettable experience.

Weeks later, it was discovered that one of the soldiers from a different unit who was a passenger aboard the *Passau* was missing. We assumed that he must have fallen over board during the commotion. About a month later, an Austrian farmer leaked information to the American authorities that he had seen the Russians burying a body near the Danube River. It was the American soldier. Negotiations were initiated to exhume and return the soldier's body to the Americans. The Russians finally agreed to release the corpse, and the assignment to retrieve the body was given to Sergeant Drushall and his hospital crew. A detachment was formed, and once again, the sergeant asked me to accompany him as the interpreter. I was leery that dressed in civilian clothes I would look conspicuous, so the same army fatigues worn by the other soldiers were provided for me to wear.

On a cool, crisp, sunny day, our convoy departed. It consisted of three vehicles--a jeep carrying the sergeant, a driver and me; a 4x4 pick-up truck with four soldiers; and an ambulance with two medics--ironically riding over the same bridge that the *Passau* had struck. We could see the Russian guards on duty and a vehicle with three other Russian soldiers waiting on the other side of the bridge, ready to inspect and accept documents to retrieve the American soldier's body. Sitting in the back of the jeep in a seat directly behind Sergeant Drushall, I was not afraid, but apprehensive. I wondered if the Russians felt the same and if they would ask any questions.

The convoy stopped. A Russian officer walked up to our jeep and accepted the papers that the sergeant presented. He told us in English, "Follow me." Returning to his vehicle, the convoy followed to an isolated farm area next to the shoreline of the Danube River. Our location was approximately ten miles south from where the *Passau* had been stranded. We were directed to a spot with a wooden marker. Four American soldiers carefully dug out the body, which was partially decomposed, covered with maggots, and emitted a horrid smell. It was a sad sight, but we were thankful that the Russians had cooperated, and I was relieved that I did not have to speak for there was no need for an interpreter. The body was placed in a plastic bag and transported to the hospital morgue, where it was officially identified as the missing soldier.

Life, once again, returned to a routine of living with my roommate, George Musil, and working at the hospital where there was a movie theater, with seating for one hundred fifty people. The theater, located on the top floor, was originally used as a training facility for Austrian nurses. Assisting the corporal who had volunteered to run the movie projector for the patients and staff, I enjoyed operating the projector and was delighted to be given the chance to view the latest American movies. When the corporal was discharged from the army and going home, he recommended that I should take his place. I quickly accepted this fun responsibility of showing movies twice a week on Tuesday and Thursday starting about seven o'clock in the evening. The USO delivered each movie to the hospital theater. A newsreel and a short comic film preempted every movie. Watching the movies increased my English vocabulary and taught me about life in America. I looked forward to seeing each film. Rita Hayward and Ann Blythe were two of my favorite actresses, and John Wayne, Douglas Fairbanks, Jr., Roy Rogers, and Clark Gable were superb actors. Their performances influenced my desire to be an American. I cannot recall specifics, but I viewed life in America as exciting with endless possibilities for the future.

The favorable experiences I had working with Americans in Austria resulted in genuine friendships and also were the basis for my positive conclusions that I truly liked Americans and that they liked me! I began dreaming about living in America someday, but my dreams faded and were replaced by duties at my regular job. My salaried position of forty hours a week dominated my time. Working more hours whenever further assignments were required, especially during emergency situations, would find me often staying past my regular forty-hour schedule. I had no time to dream about going to America. Work consumed my thoughts.

On one occasion, my team had to install a new X-ray machine, a top priority, so within twenty-four hours the machine was functioning. Staying beyond my regular time was easy for I lived across the street from the hospital, and the hospital telephone-switchboard operator had my personal extension to reach me at any time. The staff called upon me often, day and night. I did not mind for my work was appreciated. Invigorating my enthusiasm and commitment to excel in all areas, I gained confidence in this exciting lifestyle. The hospital provided a jeep for my personal use. Free meals were available at the staff mess hall, 24/7. Whenever I left my apartment, I would notify the switchboard operator of my location. The people were like family, friendly and caring with sincere concern for one another. My work knowledge and experiences advanced, and within two years, I was promoted to supervisor of maintenance for the civilian personnel.

One evening, I received a phone call about an electrical outage in the apartment of an American nurse, Annabelle, a captain who lived in the nurses' quarters. With my toolbox in hand, I set out on this job emergency. Answering my knock, Annabelle opened the door and to my surprise stood before me in a see-through negligee. Stuttering and trying to look away, I asked about the electrical problem, and she led me to her bedroom and a lamp that stood on a table next to her bed. She explained that the lamp was not working. I tried the switch, replaced the bulb, and checked the cord in that order. As I lifted the end of the cord, I chuckled for I had discovered that the plug was missing. Taking a closer look, I noticed that the plug had been cut off and a strong smell of perfume emanated from the wire. Turning around to face Annabelle, I questioned, "Why did you cut the plug?"

She smiled and confessed, "I had to find an excuse to get you to my apartment."

I was flabbergasted for I had not flirted or given Annabelle any indication that I was romantically interested, and I continued to probe, "Why me?"

"I think you are a very attractive man. I have noticed you around the hospital and would love to get to know you better."

Trying to be courteous and not encourage her, I responded that I would not jeopardize my position by getting involved with an officer, especially on hospital property, but she was very persuasive. We sat down and talked for a while over a glass of wine. Explaining that she would be completing her tour of duty soon and returning to Texas, she wanted to have a fling with a European, and I was the man who fascinated her whims. I could not refuse her tempting seduction. We made plans to meet for dinner at a quaint hotel-restaurant in town. That weekend, our rendezvous was consummated. My first experience with an attractive woman as the aggressor was strange. We met a few more times, but we never kept in touch, even though she made sure to give me her American address, and she knew mine.

The romance with Annabelle was not meant to be for I was enjoying life as a single man; yet my thoughts would often be of Renee, especially when letters were exchanged. She and her family were still residing in Vienna. They had never traveled to Rumania. Renee's parents, Ladislaus and Anna, divorced, and Anna remarried, but Ladislaus remained single for the rest of his life. He continued working in construction for the railroad. It was impossible for Renee and me to see one another because of the same problem: the Russian zone separated us. Only Austrian citizens with a picture passport were permitted to travel freely throughout Austria. As a non-citizen, Renee and I had a different picture identification stating, "A Foreign Resident of Austria." We could not cross the Russian zone. It was hopelessly frustrating! Our only means of communication was by mail. In the early part of 1949, Renee wrote to tell me that she had decided to marry an Austrian citizen. Though her decision was a complete surprise to me, I understood and wrote back my congratulations and best wishes, yet also conveyed my regrets that the circumstances did not allow us to be together.

Working for the American military occupied my mind and body. I was always busy and rarely had time to fret over or discuss personal problems in my life; however during one of my chats with Colonel Dean, the chief surgeon and commanding officer of the hospital, I happened to mention the fact that I would love to join the American Army. Colonel Dean explained, "I will highly recommend you to the authorities and investigate the possibility of your enlistment. I am a friend of General Mark Clark, the commanding general of the United States forces in Austria, and will ask him personally about the possibility of your joining."

I thanked him and admitted to myself that it would be a good opportunity for me. A few months past by, and I heard no news from the colonel. Assuming that our conversation was merely a nice gesture with no real results, I forgot about it.

When Renee was married for six months, she unexpectedly wrote about visiting me, now that she was an Austrian citizen through her marriage.

She arrived and stayed for a weekend. I introduced Renee to Rita, my new girlfriend. Arguing with Rita, Renee proclaimed that I was engaged to her first and still loved her. Two jealous women erupted like a volcano of angry words. When Rita left, I confronted Renee, insisting that she had no right to drive Rita away. I reminded Renee that she was married.

She blurted out loud, "I plan to leave my husband and return to you, if you want me? I only married to gain Austrian citizenship, so I could travel to see you and find out if we could have a life together."

Old feelings of genuine affection surfaced, and we vowed our love for each other. Renee returned to Vienna, and true to her word, started annulment procedures, declaring that her husband did not want any children.

Even before Renee's visit, my life began to change because the American military decided to relocate to a different facility. A German air force base outside of Linz was refurbished and designated as an American military base, Camp McCauley. Every building occupied by the American military, scattered throughout Linz, would be consolidated at the new air force base. The reorganization included the 124th Station Hospital where I worked and the apartment buildings where the Americans and I resided. At Camp McCauley, the hospital was renamed the 124th Mobile Army Surgical Hospital (MASH), where my new job assignment of overseeing the operations of the generators at the hospital included shift work, with twenty-four hours on duty and forty-eight hours off duty. I alternated this schedule with three other men. When working at night, each man would sleep on a cot in a room housing the controls for the generators to assure their continuous supply of electrical power to the hospital.

Prior to the major move by the American military to the new base, my parents were relocated to a refugee camp, because the barrack where they resided was only temporary housing. Since I could no longer live in the American military apartment, I applied and was granted permission to live in the new refugee camp, too. George Musil moved in with one of his relatives in Linz and continued to be employed in the same hospital that was once again named the Austrian Maternity Hospital and now completely controlled by the Austrians. My father also was transferred to work at

MASH in the maintenance section. Bus transportation was provided for all civilian workers at Camp McCauley, which was about five miles from my residence at the refugee camp. Located about two hundred yards from my front door, the bus stop was most convenient.

Before long Renee arrived, and we married on May 5, 1950, beginning our life together in the refugee camp. My parents were delighted to have a daughter in their lives, and I was truly happy to be settled down. That summer, Colonel Dean surprised me with the assurance that I would be able to join the American Army, but first I would have to go to the United States for six months of basic training and schooling. He affirmed, "After the training, I will personally request that you should be assigned to my unit."

I had never expected to hear from the colonel about the enlistment. Though I was excited about his offer, I had to be honest and consider Renee. I explained that I had recently married and the situation was different. I wanted to share the news with my wife and ask her opinion, so I could not give him a definitive answer.

The colonel emphasized, "It will be impossible to bring your wife along to America."

We both agreed that Renee should be part of this major decision.

I arrived home and told Renee the entire story. After telling her that she would have to remain with my parents for six months until my return from basic training, she sighed, "Not again! You took off for the French Foreign Legion. I thought I would never see you. Please, do not take this offer!"

I must admit that I would have immediately accepted the colonel's offer to join the American Army, but as a newlywed, I realized I had made a commitment to Renee. Respecting her feelings, my decision was to refuse his proposal. Colonel Dean understood the situation and regretfully accepted my answer.

I reflected over the possibilities that could have happened. If Renee had not returned, I would have joined the army and perhaps been deployed to Korea. Becoming involved in the serious conflict escalating in the area might have resulted in my being wounded or winding up as a casualty. One of my friends, an American medic, was killed in Korea. Another friend was seriously injured. On the other hand, joining the army could have been my ticket to fulfill my dream of becoming an American citizen. Ultimately, I reasoned that the only certainty in my life was the fact that I was headed in a different direction and that Renee and I had made a mutual decision that was the best choice for both of us based on the circumstances at that time. Only God knows the outcome of the choices we make, and as always I prayed for the best scenario.

Adjusting to the daily routines of marriage, Renee and I led a peaceful, simple life. We had no luxuries, yet managed to be very happy because we were in love. Living in a smaller barrack adjacent to my parents, our building consisted of four apartments with separate entranceways and was not equipped with running water like my parent's barrack. Our unit consisted of two small rooms. The entire apartment was about fifteen feet by twenty feet with a wall of sheet rock dividing the kitchen area from the bedroom. In the kitchen, a small two-burner, wood- or coal-fueled stove was used for cooking meals and heating the apartment, our only source of heat. An icebox for a refrigerator stood next to the doorway, and a wooden table and two chairs were against the dividing wall. The bedroom consisted of a small bed, a storage chest, and a closet that held the few clothes we possessed. An excellent seamstress, Renee used her sewing skills to create pretty curtains for the two windows and linens for the table, resulting in a warm, cozy décor. A woman's influence adds beauty and comfort to a home, no matter how small the apartment or meager the furnishings and surroundings.

Since there was no running water in our barrack, the four families shared a washing facility in an adjacent building, comprised of a room containing tubs for washing clothes. The facility also included two segregated areas; one section for men and the other for women, with latrines and showers. Using a five-gallon jug to haul water from the washroom to our apartment was the way we obtained water for drinking and cooking.

Encouraged by my parents, we cultivated a small vegetable garden in front of our unit, growing tomatoes, cucumbers, carrots, and string beans. Occasionally, we would take the bus to venture to town to shop, but most of the time it was convenient for the residents to patronize the one grocery store in the camp, purchasing food items and coal or firewood for the stove. Hardships prevailed, yet we made the best of our situation for Renee and I were together, and that was what mattered. Observing the loving behavior between my parents influenced a positive attitude in my marriage. Their affection was contagious. Love was all around.

About a year and a half later, Renee and I were happy to learn that she was pregnant, but we were concerned about providing our newborn with baby necessities. We already lived on a strict budget, but now we planned our purchases even more carefully. I bought a used crib and an oversized mattress bag, which Renee sized and sewed to fit the crib. Finding straw to fill the bag was my mission. I thought it would be an easy task, since farms surrounded the campsite. Pulling a homemade, small wagon, I set out to scout the farmland to purchase straw. Refusing my request, several of the farmers said they had none, and others angrily shouted that they would not sell anything to foreigners. To add to my dilemma, the bolt for the wheel broke off, so I carried the wagon on my back until coming to a blacksmith shop. I asked the blacksmith for a bolt to repair the wheel, and he kindly inquired about my destination.

I sadly responded, "I am desperately searching for straw for a baby's crib, and unfortunately none of the farmers want to sell their straw to me."

Feelings of sympathy seemed to surface, and the blacksmith responded, "I will repair the wheel and give you a bundle of straw free of charge." He insisted that it was a gift for the baby. The blacksmith's generous act rekindled my faith and made me realize that there will always be both good deeds and evil actions to face no matter the time or place. Relieved, I walked home with the firm resolution to teach my child to help fellow humans whenever possible. Good deeds will perpetuate more goodness.

A few weeks later on a cold, frigid day, December 16, 1952, my son was born. When Renee began labor pains, I hurried to the camp office to phone the police to send an ambulance. She delivered a healthy baby at the Women's Maternity Hospital, the same hospital where I used to work. Mother and son arrived home the day before Christmas Eve. Adorned with paper and crocheted decorations made by Renee and Mother, a small Christmas tree stood on the edge of the kitchen table. Mother cooked dinner and baked a cake. Christmas of 1952 was a memorable and blessed time for my family and me. When I placed my son in his crib on the mattress filled with straw that was given lovingly by the blacksmith, I thought of Jesus, lying in his manger of straw. I whispered a thankful prayer to Him. George Mike was the very best Christmas present anyone could have received! My newborn son brought hope and joy to the whole family. No matter how difficult the times, blessings are bestowed on us. Our son was baptized as George Mike, but Renee and I decided to call him by his middle name, Mike.

Many displaced families dreamed of going to America, but a quota on the number of people permitted to enter the United States was strictly enforced by the government. We decided to be patient and wait as long as it took for a chance to go to America. When a tempting opportunity to immigrate to Australia arose in 1951, we willingly refused, however my mother's sister and her family chose to accept the offer. They settled in the town, Paradise, in Southern Australia, near Adelaide, where Alexandria, my cousin, and her husband Paul still reside. They raised five children and are great-grandparents. They celebrated their diamond wedding anniversary on January 27, 2006, receiving congratulations from Queen Elizabeth, Major General Michael Jeffery, the governor of the Commonwealth of Australia, and other Australian government officials. It was a wise choice for them to go to Australia, for their lives were complete and fulfilled.

Several months after Mike was born, news spread throughout the camp about the arrival of Ms. Alexandra Tolstoy, the daughter of the famous Russian author, Leo Tolstoy. She and one of the founders of the Tolstoy Foundation would be interviewing former czarist officers about the possibility of relocating to the United States of America. Those men who qualified along with their families would be sponsored by the foundation to resettle in America.

The Tolstoy Foundation's offer provided a miraculous opportunity for my family. Father enthusiastically applied, carefully filling out all the forms. Ms. Tolstoy, a dignified elderly lady, interviewed each one of us, speaking fluently in Russian. Tatiana Schaufuss, another co-founder and executive of the foundation, was also present at the interviews. Ms. Schaufuss recorded everything we said. They were mainly interested in Father's military background as a czarist officer. He submitted documentation of his graduation from the Yaroslav Military Academy and of his years of service as a cavalry officer. Father showed the copies of the academy booklet and photos sent to him by the fellow schoolmate living in Paris. The information proved to be useful at the interview and pleased Ms. Schaufuss who confirmed our acceptance to the program. We were amazingly surprised that we were the only family from Camp Wegscheid to qualify.

A few months later, we were mailed instructions that we implicitly followed. First we went to the American embassy in Salzburg to process documents and receive visas to travel to the United States. Once visas were obtained, preparations for our departure began with notifying the local authorities about our upcoming emigration for clearance and approval. Next on the agenda, Father and I submitted job resignations and were given letters of recommendation to present to future employers. Finally, we began carefully packing the necessary items according to the foundation's specifications. A total of two crates about 3x3x3 feet were packed with various household or personal items. The crates would be shipped and delivered to us in America. It was our pleasure to give away other belongings to our neighbors, not only because we would be helping them, but also because this benevolent act meant leaving the camp was a reality. Concentrating totally on our move, we focused on every detail that would inch us closer to our new life in America.

In the beginning of October 1953, tickets arrived with a letter informing us to travel by train to Munich, Germany, and to report to a transfer camp for emigrants. We left two days later and arrived in Munich. We were housed in an old German Army compound; one room for my parents and brother and another room for Renee, Mike, and me. The facility was a temporary shelter for families heading in different directions. Processing our documents that included medical examinations and vaccinations took approximately a week and a half. Dissemination of information to assure that guides would meet and direct the families to their final destination was encouraging. We were not fearful of the outcome because government officials from Germany and America were competently and attentively organizing our travels. Everyone was treating us well, and we felt confident.

Emigration meant hope for the future and a better life, yet our lives would be changing again, and change for most of us is accompanied by some feelings of anxiety about the unknown. Would our new country accept us? Could Father and I find work? What would we do? Where would we live? Our concerns were eased for our family discussions stressed our determination and willingness to make every effort to succeed in America. Father's remarks echo in my ears until today, "We survived a hell on earth. Nothing can be worse than that. We finally have a chance for a decent life ahead of us. We must try to make the best of it. Let's move on."

The United States of America

O n October 20, 1953, early in the morning, we arrived at the Munich airport and boarded a chartered Trans World Airline (TWA) *Constellation*, a new, four-engine airplane. There were families on board whose final destinations could be anywhere in the United States for various organizations sponsored their migration. On this flight, our family was the only one sponsored by the Tolstoy Foundation.

The plane's first stop was Shannon, Ireland, where the passengers were asked to exit the plane during the refueling. We were allowed to stroll around in a designated section of the airport. That is where I almost got into trouble. There were two Irish police officers talking to one another. Standing near them, I overheard their conversation, but I could not determine exactly what they were saying, so I turned around and asked, "Excuse me, are you speaking with an English dialect?" Their angry looks revealed disapproval of my question.

One officer sternly answered, "It is not English, but Gaelic!" I was sorry I had ever interfered and never questioned dialects again.

The plane's next stop was Gander, Newfoundland, where once again the plane was refueled. Then, we flew onto the final stop, Idyllwild Airport (now JFK) in New York. Even though we were tired from our long day of travels, being on American soil uplifted our spirits. A representative from the Tolstoy Foundation, speaking in Russian, greeted us warmly and drove us to Grand Central Station. From there, we boarded a train to Nyack, New

York. A mini-bus awaited and took us to Valley Cottage, the estate owned by the foundation.

The seventy-five-acre estate was formally the Reed Farm located five miles north of Nyack, a city in Rockland County on the Hudson River and near Interstate Highway 9W. The Tolstoy Foundation acquired the farm in 1941 for the purpose of assisting Russian refugees. The property was now comprised of several buildings, including a dormitory and administrative headquarters with dining areas, a kitchen, and a large meeting room designated for Russian Orthodox religious services.

The estate exuded an inviting, homey atmosphere and was very different from the camp environment. Assigned to stay in two comfortable rooms similar to a dormitory, we all agreed that the new accommodations were luxurious, especially the privacy of our own bathrooms. Dinner was served in a beautifully decorated and clean cafeteria. The employees and volunteers were helpful and pleasant. All our needs were satisfied beyond our expectations.

None of us could have imagined that as a result of Father's background as a czarist officer and the sufferings he and his family endured during the Russian Revolution would lead us to America and the Tolstoy Foundation's unselfish dedication to help refugees. Our gratitude and respect for the Tolstoys and their benefactors is heartfelt, for their efforts enabled our dreams to come true. October of 1953 was a miraculous and marvelous time for all of us.

After a glorious sleep on a bed with a firm mattress that was definitely not made of straw, we ate a hardy, American-style breakfast of ham and eggs with toast and delicious tasting coffee and orange juice. At an informal meeting with Mrs. Schaufuss, we were told that we could stay at Reed Farm Valley until we found employment. My first question was, "Where is the nearest industrial city?"

"Paterson, New Jersey," was her reply. Paterson was an ideal place with many job opportunities, since emigrants from Russia and other European countries had already found employment in the numerous factories located in the city and surrounding area. Father and I were given an address of another Russian family who had immigrated to America four years before with the assistance of the foundation. They now lived in Paterson and were willing to help refugees find jobs and housing. Since Father and I had a total of fifteen dollars between us, not enough money for our job search, the extra twenty dollars given to each of us supplemented our traveling expenses and was very much appreciated.

One of the foundation's representatives literally put Father and me on the bus going to Paterson. He provided us with specific directions. We knew where to get off the bus and how to contact the Russian family volunteering to help. Father could understand English and communicate somewhat with basic expressions, but I was the only one in my family who could speak English well. Working for the United States Army enabled me to practice English language skills. Now it was my chance to put those skills to good use.

Father and I arrived in Paterson early in the morning and located the Russian family who conversed amicably and served us a delicious breakfast. After all these years, I can not recall their names and barely can recognize their faces, but I will never forget what the man told us: "In America everything is different; even the door handles are knobs that turn both ways because they are round."

Was this his way of suggesting that adjusting to a completely new lifestyle and modern way of living with unlimited opportunities would take time? Working for the Americans for six years paved the way for an easier transition for me. When I think back, Mother and Renee struggled at times, yet they adapted faster than expected.

Our Russian host accompanied Father and me to an office where we obtained Social Security cards needed for employment. Next, given directions to two factories, we were on our way. The manager of Julius Smith, a prophylactic factory in Little Falls, another town next to Paterson, hired Father because of his experience with vulcanized rubber. Needless to say, his job as a prophylactic inspector often evoked jokes and ribbing, which he laughed about good-naturedly. Father remained at the factory to fill out forms while I continued my job search at the Beatties Carpet Factory about a mile away. I was immediately hired as a machinist. Scheduled to work full time on the following Monday, Father and I were ready for our new challenges, exerting our best effort to achieve a peaceful life for our families with an economically more advanced lifestyle.

I was gleefully giddy about the speedy progress of all my expectations. There seemed to be no roadblocks in my path, and I plunged ahead. I did not want to be too cocky, so I would take time to bow my head to thank God for His unbelievable blessings. I prayed that His graces would continue to guide me in glorious America.

That evening, Father and I returned to the Russian family, who suggested that we rent the furnished apartments that were available in a building on their block, Straight Street. We agreed and put a deposit on two small efficiency apartments. Since it was too late to return to the Tolstoy estate, the Russian family invited us to stay overnight, and the next morning we began our journey back to the foundation. On the return trip, Father and I followed the clearly written directions and did not get lost, but the trip was somewhat confusing because we had to transfer to another bus. We managed to return safely and were bombarded with a stream of questions from Mother and Renee who were elated to learn that we had found employment.

Remaining on the estate for two more days was carefree and enjoyable. Particularly pleasant were the walks around the grounds. One day a merchant driving a truck filled with all sorts of fresh vegetables and ripe fruit parked in the driveway. The assortment of produce was a feast to our eyes, especially the oranges and bananas. The last time we had eaten bananas was in 1939, and everyone was eager to taste one. Father purchased a dozen bananas. Alex, born in December of 1940, had never even seen a fresh banana. Overindulging, Alex ate six in one day. Gorging on bananas caused severe stomach cramps, and his cravings for bananas were satisfied for a long time. He learned an important lesson that too much of anything is not always a good thing.

On the day of our departure, a mini-bus was provided for our family's personal transportation to Paterson, as well as more money; one hundred dollars for each family. We repaid the loan as soon as we could. We owed the Tolstoy Foundation much more than the one hundred dollars. We were indebted to them for our new lives, in a new country, and a new beginning.

The Tolstoy Foundation continues its charitable works, expanding its refugee program to include non-Russians. I have returned a few times to the estate walking along the same path to the same dormitory facility housing my family so long ago. A Russian Orthodox church was built in 1957. A library with thousands of books and rare manuscripts plus a large collection of videotapes depicting all aspects of Russian history and culture are also on the premises. This award-winning foundation has been recognized for its humanitarian principles. Alexandra Tolstoy's inspiration still flourishes through the efforts of a dedicated staff and the support of generous benefactors. May the Tolstoy Foundation continue helping needy refugees and displaced persons like my family and me.

Settling in America in our first home was exciting, even though it was merely a furnished apartment. Progression towards becoming a full-fledged American would be slow, yet steady. A place with our very own bathroom made up for the cramped quarters and tiny kitchen. Rent was forty dollars a month, including utilities.

Eagerly setting out to grocery shop at the local A&P store was another first experience for Father and me. We were overwhelmed by the amount and variety of food and beverages available. We selected purchases carefully including items like milk, bread, eggs, butter, cheese, tea, and to our amazement, jars of baby food. For about ten dollars, we carried home bags of groceries. The neighborhood stores on Broadway supplied other items to satisfy all our needs. America, a cornucopia, amazed us daily for we had done without for so many years. We had forgotten about living in a country with abundances to satisfy almost every whim. We were no longer merely existing to survive, but existing to live life to its fullest with twists and turns and changes that would move us slowly forward at first, but then eventually propel us like a rocket reaching for the moon. I felt the momentum in my mind and body. It was an exhilarating feeling. I would patiently accept the challenges with courage and conviction, for I loved being in America.

Our family began establishing a pattern or routine for our new life. At first, Renee and Mother rarely ventured outside, but gradually they explored the neighborhood, strolling around the block and eventually chancing a walk to the A & P grocery store. Each day Father and I boarded the bus to our jobs with Father's stop first and my stop, the Beatties Factory, a mile away. My job consisted of repairing machinery, mostly the carpet looms, which often malfunctioned. I began learning the techniques involved with weaving and Gerard, my boss, who was also the owner's nephew and manager of maintenance and repair, explained the factory's operations in detail.

Since other refugees were employed at Beatties, friendships were easily formed, in particular, a strong camaraderie with Hans Brauner who became my first friend in America. Hans had come to America in 1950 with Emma, his wife, a daughter and one son. Later the Brauners had two more sons born in America. Our genuine friendship brings tears to my eyes. He and his wife retired to the west coast of Florida about eighty miles north of my present residence. We were able to visit one another and reminisce about the "old times." Sadly in January of 2005, Hans passed away, but I will always remember his kindnesses as if it were yesterday. He and his family helped in so many ways.

Since Hans and his family knew what it was like to try to adjust to the unaccustomed American lifestyle, they empathized with our situation and befriended and helped us in many areas. Hans drove a new 1953 Ford Fairlane and encouraged me to obtain an American driver's license. I had maintained a driver's license in Austria that had been difficult to acquire because one had to attend classes to learn not only how to drive, but how to explain the functions of the major parts of a car, including the changing of a flat tire. A wealthy, prominent lady, who was in my driving class and owned a Mercedes-Benz, could not obtain a license. She had failed the part of the test requiring knowledge about the operation of the engine and drive shaft. She was very upset! Detailed explanations about a vehicle were not of interest or her concern, but no matter how much she complained, she could not receive a license until she passed the test. For me, obtaining an American driver's license was easy, but I could not afford to buy an automobile. Hans began driving me to work, and I contributed money to help pay for gasoline.

With his help, we moved into a full-size apartment on the north side of Paterson in a building with five other apartments. Two bedrooms, a large eat-in-kitchen, a bathroom, a living room, a den, and a balcony comprised this most suitable dwelling. Having our very own refrigerator and stove in the kitchen and a shower inside the bathtub contributed to feelings of complete satisfaction. Rent was eighty dollars a month, and this ideal lodging was worth the money. Since the families were responsible for heating their individual apartments, six steam furnaces fueled by coal were in the basement. Ordering coal to be delivered when needed and shoveling the coal into the furnace was necessary to keep the apartment warm and comfortable. Shoveling the coal before bedtime and again before heading to work were minor tasks to achieve the benefits of a cozy, warm apartment.

My family and I remained in the tiny efficiency apartment until the new apartment could be furnished. It took us two weeks to make our purchases. Patronizing a store on River Street in Paterson, I made major purchases on credit. Renee and I selected an aluminum kitchenette set, a bedroom set, a couch, lamps, and a stroller for Mike. Everything cost about two hundred and fifty dollars. Agreeing to make ten-dollar monthly payments, we were amazed when the items were delivered to our roomy apartment. Each time a payment was made, the owner of the store would record the amount in my credit booklet.

Noticing that our family was needy, one of the nicest neighbors, Ann Ruffo, not only amiably welcomed us to our new residence, but also offered us her extra blankets and towels. She mentioned our lack of basic necessities to fellow neighbors, who also generously supplied many essentials. Their kind acts and charitable gifts were accepted gratefully.

Aware of our new residence, the Tolstoy Foundation forwarded the crates we had packed in Austria. They were filled with dishes, pots and pans, utensils, and other useful objects. Once my family was established in our new apartment, Renee and I helped my parents move into a larger unit about a mile and a half from us on Mill Street in the middle of Paterson. They also purchased furniture on credit, making timely payments.

Needing extra money to pay off my debts, I started painting houses. The first house belonged to Peter, an older employee at Beatties. He paid me two hundred and fifty dollars to paint the outside of his three-story house. He supplied the paint that cost about two dollars a gallon. Using gallons and gallons of paint, it took me one month to complete the job. Painting the sides of the house was difficult because the ladder I was using was not high enough to permit me to reach the top easily. I needed to use an extension pole attached to the roller. Leaning the ladder against the side of the house, I climbed to the highest rung. Unfortunately, the angle of the ladder was not tilted enough to enable me to lean firmly against the building to be painted since the space between Peter's house and the house next door was only a few feet wide. My body weight also caused the ladder to fall against the wall of the other house. I solved the problem by bracing my foot against the neighbor's house to force the ladder to firmly lean on the house I was painting. My stance resembled an acrobat in the circus. When I finally reached the part of the house with a window, I tied a rope onto a two-by-four piece of wood and braced it inside the window. The other end of the rope was secured to the ladder, causing the ladder to prop firmly against the side of the house. Thank God, painting the front and back of the house was easier, not requiring any stunts. Satisfied with the outside paint job, Peter asked if I would paint the inside at the rate of twenty dollars per room. I agreed and painted and painted and painted!

Peter's girlfriend owned a 1939 four-door Chrysler that she no longer drove. Since she knew that buses were my main means of transportation, she offered to sell me her car for thirty-five dollars. The price was right, and I became a car owner. I was now able to arrive at my extra job earlier, not relying on the slow moving bus service.

In 2005 when touring the car museum at the Imperial Palace Hotel in Las Vegas, Nevada, a similar green 1939 Chrysler was on display. Johnny Carson, The late night host on NBC, had formerly owned this vintage vehicle and had donated it to the museum for one dollar. One always has fond memories of your very first car.

Father was impressed with my car and the independence and freedom it afforded, but he never obtained a driver's license. He relied on mass transit to get to work, but Father, Mother, and Alex would join my family for outings. Sunday afternoons were devoted to delightful drives, especially to the park in Garrett Mountain. Walking among the blooming bushes and stately trees in the fresh air was a treat. One tree was huge and must have been hundreds of years old, for its trunk was so large two men could not encircle its girth, and its lush leaves and branches touched the ground with enough room for us to comfortably stand beneath. It was like being in a gigantic tent. This was one of many relaxing Sundays together.

The extra money made from painting houses in my spare time was used to pay monthly bills, but also contributed to major purchases like a black and white television set, a popular and prized addition to our home. The TV provided entertainment as well as insights into the American culture. At first it was considered an extravagance, but eventually we could not do without it.

A more secure paying, part-time job at a gas station on McBride Avenue, where I stopped for gas, eased my money worries. Jim Lombardo, the owner, hired me to pump gas three days a week. After working at Beatties from seven thirty in the morning until three thirty in the afternoon, I would stop home to eat dinner and drive off to the gas station, working until ten o'clock. I also worked on alternating weekends from seven in the morning until three in the afternoon. Determined to improve my family's living conditions became a steadfast goal.

Being employed at Beatties was hard work, yet interesting at times, especially when called upon to help solve mechanical problems. Gerard, the manager, wanted to create a tighter weave in the carpet to prevent the threads from pulling apart. I suggested that an extra spool should be added to the loom, but the problem was the means to accomplish the task. "Weld another bracket to secure the extra spool," was my response. Successfully implementing my idea, I changed all the looms to improve the tightening and strengthening of the weave resulting in a more expensive and more durable carpet. The owner awarded me a bonus of two hundred dollars.

Gerard not only approved of my work, but also befriended me. After his father's death, he had inherited a year-round log house on the New Jersey side of Greenwood Lake. Since he already owned a beautiful home in Franklin Lakes, he decided to sell his father's property. He offered to sell the house, fully furnished, to me for nine thousand dollars. Realizing that I had no savings for the purchase, he would hold the mortgage, and I could pay whatever I could manage. It sounded like an excellent opportunity to become a homeowner, but after Renee viewed the location, she objected because it was too far away form the city and in a rural area. Even though I disagreed, I understood her opinion since she would be in the house most of the time and I would be away at work. Marriage is a partnership in which both partners should be in agreement about major decisions, so Gerard's deal was not meant to be.

On November 6, 1954, Renee and I were blessed with the birth of Carmen, a beautiful daughter, who was born in Paterson General Hospital on Market Street. Giving birth a month early, Renee had tripped and had tumbled down a few steps leading to the backyard. She was chasing after Mike who never seemed to walk slowly, but always ran around like a roadrunner. He was an energetic two-year old. Though Carmen was a month premature, she was a strong and healthy baby. Mother and daughter were both fine.

The doctor who delivered Carmen was also on the council of St. Paul Lutheran Church, where Alex attended elementary school. Becoming active in the parish, I was an usher at Sunday services and attended council meetings. At one of these meetings, the doctor announced that all council members should donate a minimum of ten percent of their salaries as a positive example for all the church members. I sincerely responded to his request by saying, "I can not afford to donate that much money at this time. My family's needs are great, but I will contribute what I can."

Displeased with my comments, the doctor proclaimed loudly, "You are not a good Christian!"

I insisted, "God will be satisfied with my offering, for He knows it is the best I can contribute."

Feeling uncomfortable, I never returned to the council meetings or that church, even though, my children and I were baptized Lutherans. Renee was a Roman Catholic. In fact, when she was a preteen, she attended a Catholic monastery school, dabbling with the idea of becoming a nun, but when her family became refugees, she attended public schools in Austria and her feelings changed. When we moved to East Paterson (renamed Elmwood Park), Mike and Carmen at first attended the public schools, but later enrolled in St. Leo Catholic parochial school because religious education was part of the curriculum. Renee and I agreed that our children should convert to Catholicism.

During the holidays, I was shopping in downtown Paterson, and I saw a sign advertising the recruitment of civil defense volunteers. During the Cold War era in America, most citizens were concerned about the threat of a nuclear attack. Never quite knowing how to repay America for accepting me and enabling my family and me to establish a life in a free society, I realized that volunteering would provide the opportunity to serve the community and America. I applied, trained, and was assigned to the Ground Observer Corps. Since radar was not available, volunteers were assigned to different observation posts. Our responsibility was to relay flying patterns of all aircrafts. Twice a week from eight o'clock in the evening until midnight, I would be stationed at the top of the YMCA building's tower, the highest point in Paterson in 1954. Using binoculars, I was conscientiously on the lookout for airplanes flying overhead. My senses were on alert. If a plane was spotted, I would immediately telephone the command center, relay my post number, and report the type of aircraft sighted and its flight direction. If I could not determine the type of plane, I would merely state that it was an unknown aircraft and specify its direction. If an unregistered flight was detected, the air force could be prepared for the possibility of an attack. After two and a half years, the observer corps was eliminated and replaced by a more efficient radar network. The observers were no longer needed; however, for our services we received a certificate of recognition from President Dwight D. Eisenhower and a lapel pin, in the shape of pilot wings with the letters GOC standing for Ground Observer Corps from the air force chief of staff. These keepsakes are still proud possessions.

In 1955 I learned from Salomon, a co-worker at Beatties, about lucrative employment with the Ford Motor Assembly Plant in Edgewater. The Ford plant would be hiring people who would eventually be transferred to the new Ford Assembly Plant in Mahwah. Salomon and I applied. On the application, I recorded that I was presently employed, but wanted to change jobs. Salomon wrote that he was unemployed. Within a week, he was accepted and started working in Edgewater. I assumed that I would never be notified, but in May of 1955, I received a letter about a job in the paint department in the old plant in Edgewater. Disappointed that the position was not in the area of mechanical maintenance, I soon changed my mind and was overjoyed when I learned about the increase in my hourly wages and excellent medical and pension benefits. I also would be able to quit my part-time job in the gas station. I decided to give notice to my present employer about my intentions to leave. Gerard was not happy and offered to increase my salary, but the amount was less than the wage quoted for the position at the Ford Company.

I enthusiastically started my first job at Ford Edgewater Plant in the commercial truck department on the assembly line, which according to the Webster's dictionary means, "an arrangement whereby each worker performs a specialized operation in assembling the work as it passed along, often on a slowly moving belt or track." I soon discovered that working on an assembly line was not an easy job. Before the parts of the truck reached my station on the assembly line, they were primed and baked. When the parts moved to my section, I worked on each piece as I walked along with the moving track for about twenty feet. My duties consisted of scuffing the left side of the truck's cap, fender, and hood, and applying a sealer to the welded joints inside the cap in less than four minutes. I repeated the process over and over again, running back to the starting point on the assembly line with no time to spare. If I had to use the bathroom, a relief man was called because the production line would not stop. Beginning work at seven, I had a fifteen-minute break in the morning, a half an hour for lunch, and another fifteen-minute break in the afternoon. At precisely four o'clock, the horn blew and the assembly line halted. Working non-stop was mentally and physically grueling. After removing my coveralls, washing my face, and scrubbing my hands thoroughly trying to wash off the sealer, I would plod to my car completely exhausted. Too tired to move, I would simply sit trying to shake my fatigue and awaken my brain before driving home. After one week of doing this tedious, boring, monotonous work, I approached the foreman, Joe Powers, and told him, "I am quitting!"

I will never forget what he said, "George, you are an excellent worker. Please, be patient. At the end of the month, our entire Ford Edgewater Plant will be moving to Mahwah, and you'll be given a better job."

I trusted his words and persevered. On May 28, 1955, I was employed at the world's largest assembly plant, the new Ford Mahwah Plant with approximately a total of seventy-five hundred employees. It was amazing! The factory in Edgewater stopped production on Thursday afternoon. On Friday, everyone reported to the new plant for orientation and assignment, and on Monday, the Mahwah plant began its first day of full production.

Joe Powers kept his promise. My main job was off the full assembly line and on the two-tone line in the truck division where specialized painting was completed. Usually these paint jobs involved different colors that needed to be separated. I would tape paper over one color specified per design. For example, sections of a postal truck or a U-Haul truck would require different colors. As soon as I taped the part, I placed it on another assembly track for the completion of the secondary painting. It was a good job. Working overtime meant that I was providing enough money to pay bills and to save for the future.

The Ford Mahwah Assembly Plant was dedicated on September 29, 1955. Accolades were extended to Henry Ford II who was the president of the Ford Motor Company since 1945. The governor of New Jersey, Robert Meyner, and other important dignitaries attended the celebration. Ford proudly announced that the Mahwah Assembly Plant was the largest in the world. He declared that in forty-eight hours the facility could be converted into a defense plant manufacturing tanks, trucks, jeeps, and other military vehicles. The thirty-eight-year-old Henry Ford II had big plans for the Ford automotive industry. I was just as proud as Ford, because I was one individual among thousands of people who was fortunate to have played a small part in the company's progressive history.

After several months of commuting to Mahwah, I needed to upgrade my automobile. Buying a used, sleek, black 1949 Buick Road Master Convertible with a straight-eight cylinder engine and luxurious red and black leather interior seemed like the ideal purchase. I paid three hundred and fifty dollars for the Buick and sold the Chrysler for fifty dollars, making a fifteen-dollar profit.

A car fit for a king, the Buick handled well in all kinds of weather, especially in snow. When I left for work on March 16, 1956, and it started to snow, I was not concerned; however, when I arrived in Mahwah, several inches of snow had already accumulated. Still snowing at noontime, there was about two feet of snow on the ground. The plant closed and the workers were sent home. I cleaned off the Buick, placing cardboard between the grill and the radiator to prevent the snow from clogging it and set off for home. I drove along my usual route through Ramsey on Route 17 heading south, but the road was impassable because jack-knifed tractor-trailers blocked the lanes. I turned the car around and headed north exiting onto Route 202, riding through Oakland and North Haledon toward Paterson.

The Buick was equipped with electro-hydraulic, powered windows. The cylindrical reservoir filled with hydraulic oil to operate the powered windows was underneath the front fender. Suddenly, all four windows slid down and were completely open. The cylinder filled with oil must have hit something causing the oil to leak and the windows to open. Not able to close them manually, the freezing wind and cold snow blew through the openings. Creeping at the speed of no more than ten miles an hour, drivers I passed looked at me as if I were crazy, shaking their heads and laughing. Luckily, I was dressed warmly, and the gas tank was full. I zigzagged on the side streets, occasionally backing up when the streets were blocked or congested. At last I arrived at the circle on Route 20 and Market Street near the Passaic River Bridge, but I could not drive around the circle because abandoned vehicles blocked my way. I decided to pull into a parking lot of a diner that was closed, sliding into a snow bank. My gas gauge registered almost empty. Leaving the Buick parked there with the windows wide open, I walked four miles home, arriving around seven o'clock   I had survived the blizzard of March 1956 that had paralyzed northern New Jersey with over three feet of snow recorded, but did my Buick survive?

The next morning was cold, but bright and sunny. Carrying a shovel, I walked back to the parking lot to find my Buick. Since the snow had not melted inside the car, I scooped it out as best I could, freed the car of snow, started it up, and dropped the car off at the repair shop. I did not go to work for two days.

Though Hans Brauner continued to work at Beatties Carpet Factory and I worked at the Ford Mahwah Assembly Plant, we still remained friends and spent good times together. Our families would meet on weekends especially in the summertime sunshine. My parents and Alex would join our outings with the Brauners at Melody Lake in Butler, a favorite place for picnicking, swimming, playing ball, and enjoying one another's company. Usually every second Saturday evening, my parents would babysit, so Renee and I could go out. Hans and Emma would join us at the German Dance Club, where couples from all over Europe gathered to dance and listen to live bands playing waltzes, tangos, polkas, foxtrots, and our favorite pop music. Forming new acquaintances with friendly conversations, we realized other families were also trying to begin new lives in America, working hard, yet finding time for merriment and celebration. Enthusiasm energized the party atmosphere for the consensus was the belief in a bright future for all refugees desiring to be good American citizens.

While still renting a house in East Paterson (renamed Elmwood Park), Hans purchased a property in Little Falls on the bank of the Passaic River. He hired a building contractor for the major construction of a four-bedroom house, while his friends volunteered to help with other chores like finishing the interior rooms with new flooring, spackling, and painting. Everyone participated, including Big Rudy, who worked for Public Service Electric and Gas Company and was the Brauners' next-door neighbor in Little

Falls. He was an expert in the area of electrical and plumbing work and knowledgeable about construction, for his house had also been newly built. A typical gathering of a few families joined forces to help out. While the children played together, the women prepared meals, and the men worked on finishing the house.

The Brauners were so grateful for the help from their friends that they hosted a 1957 New Year's Eve party in their unfurnished house before the interior was painted. The guests carried folding tables and chairs, a record player, homemade food, decorations, and other party items into the house. The once-empty house was transformed into a party palace. That evening, ten couples dressed in their best attire celebrated a very happy New Year. When their house was finished, Hans rented a truck and the gang once again pitched in, this time with the big move.

Acting on Hans's suggestion about renting his former house in East Paterson, I spoke to the landlord, Frank Ralick, and an agreement to rent was finalized. My family would be moving into a house on Franklin Avenue in a lovely neighborhood. Of course, our friends did not hesitate to help with the move. The Ralick's four-bedroom house stood at the front of a large piece of property about one hundred feet wide and two hundred feet long. The three-bedroom house I had rented was in the back of the Ralick's house and off to the side. We shared a driveway leading to the one-car garage under the right side of the house I had rented. Frank Ralick used the garage for his car, and I parked my car in a paved section partially behind his house. The remainder of the area behind both houses was a huge backyard with an in-ground swimming pool, dug out and built by Frank.

The generous and amicable dispositions of the Ralicks resulted in a genuinely close friendship. Using his backyard pool and picnic area for many fun time activities created happy memories for both families. We were also invited to their second home at the New Jersey shore on the bayside in Lavallette, where we enjoyed riding in Frank's eighteen-foot run-about. He would drive the boat, and his daughters and I would take turns water-skiing. Frank, American born of Slovak descent, treated me with warm brotherly affection. My family and I felt the same warm affection for him and his family.

By profession, Frank was a railroad policeman, but he would rather talk about his charter membership and experiences as a fireman in Company #4 in East Paterson. Our discussions inspired me to apply as a volunteer fireman. Unfortunately I could not immediately join because in 1957 there was a waiting list for volunteers for Fire Company #4, so I joined the civil defense instead. The civil defense unit was similar to the present-day emergency management department. I was assigned to the auxiliary fire department and radiological defense section. Required to attend fire academy classes for a total of eighty hours, I was qualified to participate as an auxiliary fireman. After that, I attended classes to learn the operations of a Geiger counter to monitor, detect, and handle nuclear spills. In East Paterson, I became certified as a radiological officer and in charge of a van containing equipment to detect radioactive material. Whenever a road accident involved a tractor-trailer, I was called. Dressed in special coveralls, I would race to the scene to check for radioactivity. If there was ever a nuclear emergency, I was responsible for contacting the county to dispatch their radiological response team. In two years of service, no problems were detected, thank God.

To assist Hook and Ladder Company #4, the town designated an older fire engine to my civil defense unit. The fire engine was housed in a rented garage, which was a block away from Fire Company #4. Eighteen men comprised the newly formed auxiliary unit, and the civil defense director appointed me as their chief. Our unit trained at the Passaic County fire school. Whenever there was a general alarm, we assisted with the additional fire engine. If basements were flooded, we were also notified to pump out water. Our unit was on call for all sorts of community emergencies.

Volunteering my services, not only helped my family and me to establish friendships, but also evoked feelings of acceptance and a smooth assimilation into the American culture. We loved our life in our new country and yearned to become American citizens, but a minimum of a five-year residency was required before immigrants were permitted to apply for citizenship.

In October 1958, our time had finally arrived, and all our applications were submitted. Vowing to speak English as much as possible, my mother in particular decided to attend night classes to improve her English. Father,

Mother, and Alex studied together at home.   Renee and I would also spend time reading and memorizing the important facts about American history in the booklet provided by the Bureau of Immigration. As often as possible we would all sit around the kitchen table a nd quiz each other on facts about the American Constitution, Bill of Rights, and functions of the government. Since Carmen was born in America, she was the only family member already a citizen.

On the momentous day of January 23, 1959, at Hackensack Court House, my family and I stood before the magistrate. Before we were swornin as American citizens, Father asked, "Can I change my adopted name, Prigorowski, to my biological name, Picart?" The judge had no objections and our surname was offically changed to Picart, and we finally became citizens of the United States of America. Seven-year-old George Mike Picart, dressed in a suit and tie, did not fidget and stood seriously between Renee and me. Father, Mother, nineteen-year-old Alex, Renee, Mike, and I stood proudly before the magistrate with our left hands over our hearts and our right hands uplifted in front, pledging our allegiance to the American flag and the United States of America. Afterwards, we celebrated with dinner at a special restaurant with prayers and toasts on our first day as American citizens. Since January of 1941, we had been displaced persons with no country, and eighteen years later, the best country in the world accepted and adopted us!

In the summer of 1959, I was notified that a fireman's position was available since someone had moved out of town. I was elated to accept the offer as a volunteer fireman in Hook and Ladder Company #4. Nowadays, it seems sad that priorities have changed, and a waiting list to be a volunteer is nonexistent. In fact, finding volunteers is difficult.

Although I had previously attended classes for basic firefighting, I had to complete additional training at Sea Girt Fire Academy in New Jersey. This extensive training was required and I accumulated eighty hours of courses for certification as a full-fledged volunteer fireman. I joined twenty-four other dedicated men.

In East Paterson, the community sirens were the only means of alerting the firemen. When the sirens blared during the night, the townspeople complained because sleep was disrupted. To appease the public, the members of the town council approved an ordinance that indicated the sirens would not be utilized from eleven o'clock in the evening to six o'clock in the morning. Instead of sirens, a bell, six inches in diameter, was installed next to the telephone in every volunteer fireman's house. The bell in each house would ring, non-stop, until the phone in the firehouse was answered. Living two blocks away from the firehouse enabled me to usually arrive first and answer the phone.

I laugh whenever I recall the very first time the alarm bell rang in my house. It was a summer night. The windows were open and everyone was sleeping peacefully. When the loud, continuous bonging sounds erupted from the living room where the telephone was located, Renee and I sprang out of bed with heart failing fright. We thought we had prepared ourselves for the sound of the bell alarm, but we had not realized how the clamoring bell sounded in the stillness of night. The loud ringing bell seemed to last forever. Our neighbors were also awakened and baffled, until the circumstances were explained. Surprisingly after a while, the children seemed to adapt to the loud bongs, sometimes sleeping right through the noise. Renee was not pleased, but simply endured the commotion.

Rushing to the firehouse as quickly as possible to stop the clamoring bell was a definite incentive for every volunteer fireman. I was especially organized during the wintertime for I arranged my clothes in preparation for an alarm. My shirt was on the chair near the bed. My pants were on the door handle. My turn-out coat hung over the stair railing, and my boots were on the bottom step. Awakened by the bell alarm, I would quickly dress as I ran down the stairs and out the door to my car, that was always facing the street, so I did not have to back down the driveway. Once the phone at the firehouse was answered, the bell in each house would cease ringing. Then, I would receive and record the message about the address and type of fire onto a blackboard. Opening the overhead door for the hook and ladder fire truck, I would start the fire truck's engine, drive onto the apron of the firehouse, and wait for a minimum of three other volunteers before racing to the fire.

The volunteers at Hook and Ladder Company #4 respected the mutual aid understanding among firemen and assisted in fighting fires in nearby towns. A strong camaraderie and bonding emerges between and among firefighters. Their relationships form a true brotherhood. I was personally involved in responding to many fires throughout the years. One happened in a lumberyard on Market Street in Saddle Brook, a town next to East Paterson. The facility was engulfed in flames, and the firemen in Company #4 responded, discovering that a lack of water pressure was a problem. As a result, both fire departments joined forces to tap into East Paterson's hydrants and to pump water from the Passaic River. Their combined efforts prevented the fire from spreading.

Another incident occurred when a general alarm was sounded and all fire companies in town responded to a serious fire on Christmas Eve at a gas station on the corner of Market Street and the Boulevard. The cause of the fire was carelessness. While a car was on the lift, the mechanic was trying to repair a leak in the gas tank. Gas was dripping onto the floor causing a puddle. The droplight he was using was not secured properly and fell, breaking the bulb, and igniting a fire. Fortunately, the mechanic escaped without harm, but the inside of the station was engulfed in flames. The outside temperature was below zero making it difficult for the water from the hydrant to flow. The water was turning into ice and the icy spray hit our faces causing frostbite. We had to use chemical foam to extinguish the fire. When we returned to the firehouse, many of us, including me, looked like green monsters from the frostbite. Medical treatment was required. Those who are not involved in firefighting may not always be aware of the dangers and stress that firefighters encounter. Firefighters are dedicated to save lives and properties, and the citizens in the communities should appreciate their unselfish and brave efforts.

All fire departments try to educate the public about fire prevention. The message, in particular, is emphasized to the youth in the community during fire prevention month each October. Using vacation time that permitted me to miss a day of work without losing a day's salary, I joined fellow firemen to visit the schools in town to teach fire safety and explain the duties of firemen. From Hook and Ladder Company #4, four firemen, including me, were assigned to St. Leo parochial school, where Mike and Carmen were enrolled as students. The students and faculty were already outside awaiting our arrival for a demonstration. After the driver parked the fire truck, he secured the out rigs to keep the truck stable. The ladder was in the horizontal position enabling me to run to the top rung of the ladder. While I sat on the top rung, another firefighter positioned himself to operate the hydraulic motor to raise the ladder. Giving him a signal, he raised the ladder and lifted me to a height of seventy-five feet to the top of the church roof. Another fireman, standing near the students and faculty, explained in detail the operational procedures of the demonstration they were witnessing. While on the ladder, I noticed several small balls in the gutter. Retrieving them, I threw them to the ground and the children ran after the bouncing balls. Not realizing that my actions would cause a disturbance, I hoped that the students who had left their places to fetch the balls would not be reprimanded. Once they settled down, we continued the program with fire prevention and safety rules. Later, one of the nuns approached and exclaimed to me that she and the students were impressed with and thankful for our fire prevention program. She also mentioned that my son had boasted out loud, "That's my father on top of the ladder!" That evening, Carmen and Mike bragged all night about my daring feat. It was the big event of the week! Important lessons taught in a fun situation have a lasting effect.

Aware of my interest, enthusiasm and dedication in fire prevention, the fire chief in East Paterson asked me to become a fire prevention inspector, attending seminars at Rutgers University in New Brunswick and Sea Girt Fire Academy for certification. I happily accepted. Completing the requirements, I became a fire inspector for a few months until June of 1964.

When I purchased a house in Paramus, New Jersey, I had to resign my position since I would no longer be residing in East Paterson. I was sad to leave and knew I could not stay away from volunteering as a firefighter, so I contacted the fire chief in Paramus. Once again, I was informed of a waiting list. The chief's son was next in line, but because of my years of experience, I could have displaced his position. Realizing that the chief earnestly wanted his son to be on the fire department, I decided to wait for the next opening.

One of my neighbors in Paramus was a police captain on the Paramus force. He told me about the need for police reservists, a volunteer group who assisted the regular police in the traffic division and in the court as bailiffs. Since I had not heard from the fire chief in three months, I applied as a police reservist, was accepted, and trained at the Bergen County Police Academy. Sworn in as a member of the Paramus Police Reserves, I volunteered monthly for a minimum of twenty hours, working on patrol duty and as a bailiff. After several months of exemplary service, I was included in a group of special police reservists who were paid for traffic details or crowd control for town events like parades, athletic games, and carnivals. A year later I was contacted about the availability of a fire position, I declined in favor of staying with the police reserves.

Working at the Ford plant and volunteering as a police reservist were not the only jobs keeping me busy. I also started redecorating my three-bedroom, split-level house. My first project was refinishing the basement into a unique family room. The existing family room, adjacent to the garage, was smaller than the basement and needed to be used as a sewing room for Renee. She was an accomplished seamstress creating stylish outfits for Carmen, herself, other family members, and friends. The basement was the only area left that could be made into a more suitable recreation room for the entire family.

Always admiring the beauty of the Hawaiian Islands, redoing the family room with a tropical theme was my plan. I started with covering three of the walls with surf-wood paneling. I covered the fourth wall with sheet rock and canvas on which Father painted a mural of a beach on the island of Kauai in Hawaii. Using oil paints, he copied the picture from a post card, enlarging the scene to encompass the entire wall that measured seven and one-half feet by eighteen feet. Stapling white tiles to the ceiling beams was next, followed by the installation of a tile floor that looked like pebble stones in three dimensions. To accentuate the mural's lifelike qualities, I positioned indirect lighting over the scene. On the opposite side, I built a bar nine feet long, with a mirror as wide as the bar hanging on the wall behind it and reflecting the painting of the Kauai Beach mural. When sitting at the bar and looking into the mirror, one would swear, the palm trees and sandy beach with the rippling waves of the Pacific Ocean were a realistic scene directly behind you.

The four support columns in the basement were changed into coconut palm trees. Ordering the palm bark from a company in Florida was my first step. The next process was to wire the bark around each column and then attach artificial palm leaves to the top of the tree. Fastening four or five coconuts underneath the leaves completed the transformation. Bamboo furniture; a couch, two side chairs, lamps, a large glass table, and five bar stools with leopard-like seat covers, completed the tropical theme. A sound system, with controls behind the bar, consisted of a record player and a radio. The basement had undergone a complete metamorphosis into a tropical paradise.

Since the inside of the house no longer needed to be renovated, my attention focused on the outside. I wanted to construct an in-ground pool, but because of the septic system, underground pools were not permitted. Several months later, the new sewer system was installed on the north end of Paramus where I lived, so I seized the chance to begin preparing the backyard for the installation of an in-ground pool. Shopping carefully, I hired a company to install a 24- by 36-foot pool for nineteen hundred dollars. The price sounds unbelievably inexpensive compared to the cost of pools today. The pool was nine feet at the deepest end and four feet at the shallow end. When I had the pool built, the Borough of Paramus had no formal directives about pool construction, but soon after written ordinances restricted the size of pools on certain properties. My pool would have been much smaller. Hiring a mason, a cement walkway, surrounding the pool, was completed. The walkway was connected to the existing 20- by 40-foot patio. Although existing bushes separated my property from my neighbor's land, I installed a chain-linked fence about four feet high around the perimeter of the backyard for safety and privacy. Landscaping added the finishing touches, when I planted several mimosa trees with white and pink fragrant blooms along the fence. These exotic trees contributed to the beauty of the surroundings. Family and friends spent joyful times together at the pool and in the tropical family room.

After Alex had graduated from high school, he agreed with my suggestion to work with me at the Ford Mahwah Assembly Plant. Progressing to an inspector after about five years, he continued working on the shift from four in the afternoon to midnight. A carefree bachelor until he married in 1967, he and his bride rented an apartment in Paterson in the same building where our parents resided. A year later, Susan, his only child, was born. Providing housing for his family and his mother-in-law and grandmother-in-law, Alex purchased a two-family house in Paterson.

Before Alex married, he joined the police auxiliary in the city of Paterson accumulating seventeen years of service and like me achieving the rank of deputy chief. An avid gun collector for most of his adult life, Alex joined pistol leagues through the years, developing into an expert target shooter and achieving numerous trophies and awards. In fact, we participated in many of the same target shooting competitions and were invited to compete at the United States Eastern Regional Matches at the Secret Service Academy in Beltsville, Maryland. Alex's ultimate achievement was ranking as third in the New Jersey Governor's Top Twenty Shooters and becoming an instructor for the National Rifle Association. Completing courses to become a gunsmith contributed to his knowledge and expertise with all sorts of firearms, and when he left Ford Mahwah Plant, his knowledge enabled him to accept a job as a gunsmith in the Navy Arms Company, advancing to the position of plant manager.

Alex divorced in 1987 and remarried in 1989. He and his wife, Arline, are retired and are happily living in Arizona, the perfect place to pursue his interests in firearms and leather crafting. Competing at the Cow Town Cowboy Shooters Association in Fort Snow, Arizona Territory, the Arizona Police-Fire Games, or the Annual World Championship of Cowboy Action and Wild West Jubilee, he is known as "Dead Eye Al." Fellow club members appreciate his superior workmanship on repairs and modifications of guns.

All Cow Town shooting matches take place on a range that replicates a town in the Wild West where all shooters are required to be dressed in authentic western clothing. Jokingly, I often say that Alex was born too late! He should have lived during the days of the Wild West, because he definitely enjoys the lifestyle of a gun-slinging cowboy.

Though Alex and Arline are many miles away in Arizona, we communicate constantly through e-mails, phone calls, and visits as often as possible. Utilizing his talents with technology, Alex records special events on DVD/video, customizing and producing a splendid account of his personal and family events. After viewing his productions, it seems that we are together again. Alex is the best younger brother, an older brother could ever wish for. We love one another dearly!

When Mike and Carmen were older, Renee began working for an exclusive dress shop, Marcia's, in Teaneck. Her working hours would be scheduled during the children's school time on weekdays. She would occasionally work on Saturdays. The money saved from Renee's employment, enabled us to sponsor her brother, George, his wife Ilse, and their daughter, little Renee, to live in the United States. Paying for their plane fare and other expenses, the family arrived from Vienna in the summer of 1965. Their presence reminded us of our first time in America, and my family was pleased to assist with anything needed. They moved into our house until George found a job and an apartment. Since George was a master tailor, he had no trouble finding a position in an elite men's department store in Ridgewood. Renting an apartment a few blocks from the store was most convenient. Soon after, I taught him to drive, and George purchased a used car to obtain more independence and mobility.

After a few years, George rented a store located in Ho-Ho-Kus for his own tailoring business. He financed money for his new establishment by taking out a business loan to purchase sewing machines, yards of material, mannequins for the window displays, and furnishings. Of course, Renee and I contributed monetarily once again, and I worked diligently helping to remodel the store. Implementing our decorating plans as quickly as we could, George and I created a luxurious interior of oak paneling with recessed arches of red velvet. Divided into two sections by a wall and a red-curtained doorway, the back part of the store became the workshop, and the area in the front was transformed into a showroom, servicing the customers. I built a counter, private dressing booths, shelves that held rolls of material, and a platform that stood firmly on the floor in front of a seven-foot high tri-sectioned mirror. Lush red carpeting was installed. Life-size sculptures and floral arrangements were placed in prominent areas next to several solid red or black leather swivel chairs. The store conveyed an atmosphere of elegance. "Your Measure & Make Shop" was the name of George's tailoring business. At first George's tailoring store merely attracted customers requiring clothing alterations, but soon his work progressed to custom-made outfits, his specialty. The customers would select fashions from various design books placed on counters and tables. One popular design for men was the Nehru suit.

On one occasion, I witnessed a gentleman arriving at the tailor shop in a chauffeur-driven Rolls Royce. When he took off his jacket to try on the custom-made suit designed by George, it was obvious that his back was hunched. After adjusting the suit jacket, his hunched back seemed to disappear, and after several turns in front of the mirror, the gentleman smiled and ordered a half dozen more suits. My brother-in-law later explained that he had used padding to balance the appearance of the back deformity. It worked! The price for each suit was one thousand dollars.

Business flourished because of George's superior tailoring skills. His success continued to grow along with his family. He and Ilse had more children, two sons, Steven and Jeffrey. They could afford to rent a house in Paramus. Tailoring orders were overflowing, so much so, that he hired a seamstress to assist with the workload. Life seemed to be going well, with another American dream fulfilled. George's income was at its peak, however, the more money he made, the more foolish his decisions about spending. He began partying, overdrinking, womanizing, and neglecting family and business responsibilities, until he fell deeply into debt.

Renee and I had no inkling that his extravagant life style had resulted in severe financial problems, until the day he stopped to say good-bye. He and his family arrived at our house in their new Chevrolet station wagon. Running away from the creditors, they had packed their car with as much as it could hold. The children were sandwiched between mounds of packages and suitcases. A rack secured on the car's roof held more possessions. Renee, inflamed with anger and devastatingly sad at the same time, pleaded with them to stay. We promised to help them, but our reasoning statements were useless, for George was a strong-willed man who could not be swayed. He vehemently enforced his rules and decisions upon his wife and children. They followed his demands implicitly. It was 1972, and George and his family left New Jersey and headed west to California. About two months later, he phoned from New Mexico because he had run out of money. We wired money to him. After awhile George acquired a job as a tailor, but his family unit fell apart, and he and Ilse divorced.

About a year before George had died at the age of sixty in 2001, we had a chance to meet after not seeing one another for nearly thirty years. His handsome appearance was stylish and impeccable, for his flare for fashion had not diminished, and his good looks prevailed. Once again, he was employed as a tailor in a major department store. Greeting one another with a huge bear hug, he cried and thanked me for trying to help him through the years. He apologized repeatedly for his past mistakes and bad decisions. I believe he had regretted his actions. Whatever his life's choices, I am not the one who will be the judge, for George may have done things that were disappointments to others, but he also hurt himself as well.

When my son Mike was seventeen and a half years old in 1969, he joined the navy during the Vietnam War and completed basic training in Michigan at the Great Lakes Naval Base. He was then assigned to the 46th Attack Squadron based at the Lemoore Naval Air Station near Fresno, California. Transferred onto the aircraft carrier the USS *Midway*, Mike was deployed to Vietnam. It was not my destiny to fight in Indochina with the French Foreign Legion in 1946, but ironically it was my son's fate to fight in Vietnam years later to carry on the Picart military presence, a legacy I would not have chosen to pass onto him.

A squadron clerk, Mike was responsible for keeping records about the pilots and planes aboard the carrier, meticulously logging the flying time and pertinent statistics about each pilot and aircraft. Another important duty was being part of the helicopter crew to rescue downed pilots. After serving about eighteen months in Vietnam, the USS *Midway* was scheduled to return to the port in San Diego, but the replacement carrier, the USS *Wasp*, developed mechanical problems, therefore, the crew on the USS *Midway* was reassigned an additional tour of duty. The crew performed admirably, even when their length of duty time was extended. Travels during his time in the navy included stays in China, Japan, Hawaii, and the Philippines. Awarded several medals and commendations that Mike never talks about leads me to believe his military experiences were not always pleasant or easy. I am grateful that our family's prayers were answered, and he returned home safely. I am as proud as he is of his honorable navy service. Mike achieved the rank of petty officer first class. Discharged from the navy in 1974, Mike decided to live in California for a year. Upon his return, he chose to join Alex and me, working at the Ford Mahwah Plant. His employment enabled him to rent a house in Caldwell and to live on his own.

Graduating from Paramus High School, Carmen continued her education earning certification as a court stenographer; however, she was unable to obtain a position in this field. She accepted employment as a legal secretary instead, with a law firm in Wood-Ridge. Carmen continued to live at home.

My parents moved to a senior citizens apartment building located on River Street in Paterson in 1974. Though growing older, Mom and Pop maintained excellent health and vitality and were able to continue to live independently. My brother and I would visit regularly, and usually on most every Sunday, they would spend the day at my house in Paramus. Keeping busy, Mother cooked, crocheted, and sewed, while Pop perfected his painting skills. He became a prolific artist and sold many of his creations at local exhibitions. His paintings reflected portraits, still life, and landscapes of present surroundings, but also fond places in Austria and Lithuania.

One of my favorite paintings is of Cathedral Square in the center of Vilnius, highlighting the ancient tower that was built in the thirteenth century. We had lived two blocks from this historic site. Born and raised in Vilnius until I was thirteen years old, I would often walk by the tower, but I had never been inside because it was usually locked securely and off limits to the public. I recall being told that in medieval times this fortress was the main lookout point to alert the townspeople of advancing enemy troops. With many openings at each level, the huge round-shaped tower stood majestically in the center of the town square reaching toward the sky. It was the tallest structure in Vilnius. A cupola with four large openings--one facing in each direction of north, south, east, and west--encompassed the top level with a gigantic clock atop each of the four openings. Everyday a soldier carrying his trumpet would climb the steps to the cupola. At the stroke of noon, he would play a tune, tooting his horn in each direction, so the melody could be heard loudly and clearly throughout the city. This ritual of the trumpet player signaling noontime is especially vivid when I look at my father's painting.

As Pop grew older, he painted less and less, because he could not tolerate the offensive smells of the paint thinner and oils. Other fun pastimes replaced painting like reading, listening to music, playing cards, dancing occasionally, and playing chess with Alex or me. Mom and Pop had an unusual way to watch television in the living room. Each of them sat facing in opposite directions to view TV programs from two separate televisions. This peculiar arrangement worked for them because they adored being together, even though they could not agree on programs to watch.

My parents were married almost fifty years. After all those years, their marriage was a loving relationship. They were rarely apart, enjoying a faithful friendship and romantic love. Seeing them together always made me smile and think about my own marriage. It was time for Renee and me to concentrate on our life together, since our children were establishing independent lives and needing us less and also since I felt we seemed to have grown apart. We had celebrated our silver wedding anniversary in 1975; yet I intuitively sensed that Renee seemed dissatisfied and melancholy at times. Whenever I tried to communicate my concerns, she would not acknowledge any problem, dismissing my inquiries with a curt, "No, nothing is wrong." No matter what she said, I sincerely felt there was a communication problem. I mentioned my concerns often, until she finally agreed to attend marriage counseling, but unfortunately after the first session, she refused to attend any others. Living with Renee for twenty-five years and not knowing what she really was feeling or thinking was frustrating. We usually came to mutual agreements, with no conflicts, but I still felt that something was not right. I was willing to try anything to bring us closer together. I had already resigned my position with the police reserves, and Renee was no longer working full time, only sewing professionally for a few customers, so we had time to regain intimacy. I suggested a month vacation in Germany and Austria, not only in celebration of our anniversary and renewal of our love, but also to visit Renee's family and my friend, George Musil. Perhaps going back to the past would help us communicate better about the future.

Flying to Frankfurt/Main, Germany, in the summer of 1975 was exciting. A taxi ride to Marburg, where Lilly, Renee's widowed sister resided, was our first stop. Though the sisters communicated regularly, they had not seen one another for over twenty-five years, so their reunion was joyous with incessant chattering, mostly from Lilly, the loquacious sister, rather than Renee, the more reticent sister. Renee was also happy to become reacquainted with her paternal aunt and uncle, retired professors from the University of Berlin, who had visited us in America a few years before.

Since Germany is a country with many castles, next on our agenda was a tour of a medieval castle in Marburg, where I photographed every section, especially the exhibits in one room that contained treasures given to the king of Marburg from the emperor of China. One precious gift was a life-size buddha made of jade. With the flash on the camera working precisely, I snapped about five photographs. When the film was developed, all the photos were visible except for the five photos taken in the room with the Chinese exhibits. After discussing the situation with Renee and Lilly, we were not able to formulate a reason for the undeveloped photos, but we did express experiencing strange sensations when viewing the Chinese treasures. Renee recalled feeling cold, and I explained an uneasy feeling as if someone were watching me. Lilly reminded us that the tour guide mentioned that workers reported seeing ghostly figures roaming through the rooms. I do not believe in ghosts, yet this particularly strange outcome of the photos not developing was a phenomenon with no logical explanation. If we had more time, it would have been interesting to further investigate the causes for the blank negatives.

Lilly accompanied us on other sightseeing tours and recommended dining at her favorite restaurants, especially one place specializing in Italian cuisine. The menu was extensive and the food was delicious, until the time I ordered a pizza. It was more like a deep-dish pie filled with cheese and very little tomatoes and sauce. The owner of the restaurant announced that his wife had given birth to a baby boy, so I gave him an American Silver Dollar coin as a good luck token for his newborn son. Delighted with my gift, he reciprocated with glasses of an Italian brandy called grappa for each of us. Grappa is made from the distilled sediment left over after pressing the grapes to make wine. Its taste is similar to strong, German schnapps.

When we said our farewells to Lilly at the train station, she promised to visit us in America, and she did come in 1995. Next on our itinerary was boarding the famous Orient Express train heading for Vienna, stopping at major cities like Wiuzburg, Nurenberg, Regensburg, and Passau. Since our journey would require an overnight stay, our accommodations were in a sleeper cabin comfortably equipped with a private bathroom, a couch that converted into a single bed, with another pullout bunk bed overhead. Excellent meals and beverages were served in the dining car. We arrived in Vienna the next day and stayed with Renee's mother, Anna, and her second husband, Emil. Our visit enabled us to reminisce and share family stories in person, because we had not seen Anna since her visit to America in 1958. We showed photographs of Mike in his navy uniform, a handsome young man, and Carmen, an attractive young lady, who reminded Anna of her daughter, Renee. A few months after Mike was born, Renee had traveled to Vienna to introduce her parents to their new grandson. Unfortunately, that was the only time Ladislaus had seen his grandson. Renee's father had died a year before our visit to Vienna. The reunion was relaxed and enjoyable, but too short. We had to move on.

Renting a Mercedes, Renee and I resumed our trip heading for Linz. We would be staying with George Musil and his family at their beautiful house in Poeslingberg for a few days, and then use the rest of the time to vacation together, touring places from our past.

Daily excursions with the Musils disclosed a reconstructed Linz with not a trace of wartime damage. Several old landmarks, the churches and the special monument in the middle of the city square that recorded the number of people who had perished during the time of the Black Plague, remained the same, but most of the other structures had either been rebuilt or newly erected. Many places I saw jogged my memory, for they were unrecognizable to me. The visit to Auhof, the refugee campsite that used to be my family's residence for many years, was completely transformed into middle-class apartment complexes. The Hermann Goering Iron Factory, where Father had worked during the Second World War, had been completely rebuilt and changed back to the original Austrian Iron Works. The Allied Forces had bombed the factory because of the production of German tanks.

Renee and I were pleased to view a peaceful, charming Austria. We also stopped at the cemetery to pay respects to Grandfather and Grandmother Fuchs. A simple wooden cross marked their graves at this unembellished burial site. I silently prayed for the repose of their souls and thanked my two loving grandparents for the goodness in their lives and their loving support.

Continuing our journey and following the Musils' car, we drove by the hospital, the very same hospital, where George and I had been employed and where Mike had been born. I almost could see myself as a young man walking to my apartment, after a tiring day of work at the hospital. Years of employment with the American Army contributed to my confidence, happiness, and eventual success. My memories of the camaraderie, mutual respect, loyalty, and cooperation among the military personnel surfaced. Those influential years of a hard-working refugee were the foundation for a new life in America.

The next stop on our travels was revisiting the Wofgangsee (lake) at Waisses Roessel Inn (White Stallion Inn), where George and I often skied. It was particularly wonderful, rekindling more memories of our skiing vacations in the nearby Alps. Though there was no snow on the mountain for our visit, we enjoyed the scenic views, the scrumptious meals, especially my favorite apple strudel, and the steamboat ride around the lake.

An outing to Salzburg, where years earlier the movie, "The Sound of Music," was filmed, became our next attraction. Attending the performance of Jederman, a musical play performed in the courtyard of an ancient castle, was the highlight of our visit to Salzburg. Microphones were not used because the acoustics were perfect. The slightest whispers could be clearly heard. After our stay in Salzburg, Renee and I bid a fond farewell to our dear friends, the Musils, for their vacation time was over and George had to return to work. It was an emotional parting for all of us.

Renee and I then traveled to Gmuden am Traunsee, where we had honeymooned. The town of Gmuden is on the lake of Traunsee. The mountain called Traunstain sits on the south side of the lake. My eyes focused at the top of the mountain and traveled slowly down the side, until reaching the bottom, where the mountain seemed to fall into the lake. The view is even more breathtaking in the winter when the mountain is covered with snow. The Gasthaus (inn) where we stayed was on the lake to the left of the mountain. Unbelievably, the inn had not changed in twenty-five years. Time seemed to have stood still. Registering us for the same room we had slept in so many years before, the same proprietor recalled our names and honeymoon stay. The same dark, oak furniture decorated the lobby, the formal dining room, and the bedroom. Adjacent to the lake, the patio restaurant had the same type of white and red striped umbrellas mushroomed over the round wooden tables. Renee and I had gone back in time. Our surroundings were very much the same as in 1950, yet we were older and two very different people.

Realizing that our month-long vacation was over, Renee and I drove back to Vienna to spend one last day with Anna. The following morning we arrived at the Wesbahnhof station to board a train to Frankfurt and then on to the airport. During the long flight to New York, our conversations were casual and uneventful without any discussion about our true inner feelings. I did not probe or debate or delve into my serious thoughts for deep down I knew that our vacation in the summer of 1975 did not bring Renee and I closer together. The trip was glorious at all levels except the important area, an intimate renewal of love.

After a few weeks at home, Renee's discretions were secretive. Once again, her actions obviously proved to me that something was truly wrong in our marriage. At times when I walked into a room and she was on the telephone, Renee would suddenly stop talking and announce that she would return the call later. Arranging more frequent luncheon dates with her girlfriends and spending time creating a meticulous appearance made me suspicious. I would phone her at home, and she was not there. When I inquired about her whereabouts, she would always say, "I was out with the girls," contributing no further information. Further questioning was useless, for her answers were always the same. Renee's two pals were divorcees who usually declared in my presence that they loved the freedom of not being married.

Renee's suspicious behavior caused me to investigate her actions. I was bitterly upset, but not surprised when I discovered that she was having an affair with a married man, an acquaintance of one of her girlfriends. Renee and I had been through tough times together and finally achieved the American dream, yet life with me was no longer significant to her. I was disappointed, but I did not want to discard my love and twenty-five years of marriage, so I confronted her about seeing another man. She denied having an affair. Even though I knew she had cheated, I asked if she would try to save our marriage and seek help by going back to the marriage counselor with me. She agreed and we attended one session together. The counselor, who was a certified psychologist, spoke to each of us separately and set up an appointment for the following week. When the time came to return for our session, Renee proclaimed that she did not like the counselor and suggested that I should go alone.

The realization and the acceptance of the fact that I could not continue to be married under these distrustful circumstances, with loss of respect for the woman I loved, overwhelmed me. I firmly announced, "I am filing for divorce!" Insisting that she would not agree to a divorce, I explained that proof of the affair would be disclosed. When I mentioned specific details, she realized that her denials and refusals were useless. We mutually agreed to dissolve our marriage amicably and divide our money and possessions equally. Later her lawyer tried to obtain more money, but to no avail.

I contacted a realtor and regretfully put my house up for sale. It was sold in one day! Changes in my life and my family's life sped ahead like a car with no brakes. At twenty-one years of age, Carmen moved into her own apartment in Wallington, and Renee moved nearby in the same apartment complex. Most of the furniture in the house was divided between them, and I helped with both moves. Then I concentrated on my move. Boxes of clothes, a desk, a dresser, and some mementos were put in storage because the garden apartment in Saddle Brook, where I would be living, was not available until the first of September. Moving temporarily to the Red Carpet Inn on Route 17 in Paramus for one month was a practical decision, but a strange and lonely experience. I became depressingly sad. I had left a family and a home that were not only symbols of status, dignity, hard work, and pride, but also fond memories of joy and love. Feeling like an actor performing in a bad play, I looked physically the same when I stared in the mirror, but I did not recognize the real me. All sorts of questions reverberated in my mind, but no answers satisfied my queries. Restless, sleepless nights caused anguish and distress. Feelings of sorrow and loneliness led to deeply depressing thoughts of life not worth living. Was this sad existence my reward for relentless efforts to provide a good life for my family? I had worked hard and done my best. Life seemed unfair.

When I finally moved to my apartment in Saddle Brook, I tried to convince myself that I was feeling better, but I truly was not happy. A few days later on my birthday, September 4, 1976, I turned forty-nine. It was the worst birthday in my life, even more devastating than when I turned twelve and Poland was invaded. What could I do to improve my attitude? I needed to snap out of this depression. Who could help me? My parents became my inspiration, devoting hours of caring conversations that eventually helped alleviate my gloominess. Once I realized that happiness is much more than a place or situation or another person or possession and that it starts within each individual, my outlook became positive. If Mom and Pop could lose so much during their lifetime and still smile, I could, too. I decided to move on and begin a new life again.

Years later when I could reflect about the divorce more objectively and without sad emotions, I realized that the failure of my marriage not only troubled me, but affected my children. I assumed that since Carmen and Mike were in their early twenties that they were old enough to handle the divorce, but I later felt that their lives were somewhat shaken and scarred. After a while, they managed to cope, for their roots were embedded in a loving and strong foundation. Thank God, they both continue to be independent, smart, and hard-working adults, who have established successful lives and loving relationships. My only regret is that when they both needed me, I could not comfort or ease their hurt for my own pain flooded my mind with tormenting questions about causes for the break up. Carmen and Mike may have asked themselves the same question that swirled around inside my head, "Why did it all happen?" It is a difficult question to answer. I blamed Renee. I blamed myself. I eventually resigned to the fact that no matter what the reason or reasons, I would not look back, but move forward. I learned to try to make good decisions and persevere in life's struggles, especially communicating openly and honestly in all my relationships. Human mistakes can haunt and torment forever.

My new life as a bachelor began with the first major decision to take a six-month leave-of-absence from work. I booked a sixteen-day cruise, mostly for singles, that would be sailing from New York to the Virgin Islands, Venezuela, Curaçao, Aruba, and Bahamas. Was I running away from my heartache? What exactly was I looking for and what would I find? Whatever would happen, I was determined to explore different places and meet new people. I would try to forget the bad occurrences from the past and seek to rekindle happiness.

On a cold February day, Carmen joined me for a bon voyage party on board the *Oceanic*, a Home Lines cruise vessel, staffed mostly with an Italian crew. The ship was most glamorous.

Carmen and I toured the ship, and then returned to my cabin to munch on hors d'oeuvres and drink champagne. An announcement directed the visitors to disembark, signaling that the ship would be leaving port. The non-travelers assembled onto the dock waving farewell and best wishes for a wonderful trip. Spotting Carmen in the crowd waving to me, I waved back and considered myself blessed and fortunate for a caring daughter. Though Mike could not join me that day, the supportive sentiments he had expressed were also much appreciated. My children encouraged me to sail off in search of adventure, fun, and happiness. Mom and Pop also approved of my actions. In fact, they were rarely judgmental or expressed surprise about my decisions. Their comments were usually reassuringly positive.

Partying on board the *Oceanic* continued as the ship left Pier 54 and cruised down the Hudson River. The ship passed the New York skyscrapers, Ellis Island, the Statue of Liberty, and finally under the Verrazano Narrows Bridge, heading into the Atlantic Ocean. Years later, the *Oceanic* had been transformed into "The Big Red Ship," catering to families that combine a stay at Disney World in Florida and time on a cruise ship. No matter how I try, I cannot adjust to the magnificent *Oceanic* being painted red.

Excitement about my first cruise felt similar to my feelings when coming to America, uncertainty about the outcome, but a willingness to try my best for the ultimate goal, a better life. The same trepidations that any human might experience when trying something new surfaced in my mind, but I ignored them because determination overpowered my anxieties, so I concentrated on comparing my cruise to the fun times on the *Passau*. Chimes rang and interrupted my thoughts. It was time for the first seating for dinner at exactly six o'clock

Dressed in the required formal tuxedo, I left my room and headed for the dining room. I followed the maitre d' to my assigned table, where I was the last person to be seated. Two brothers, Kurt and Hans from Connecticut; a husband and wife, John and Barbara; a young lady, Cherie, from Suscachuwa, Canada; and I were meeting for the first time. The steward presented an extensive menu to each of us. I tried to concentrate on the names and descriptions of each item, but the day's events cluttered my thoughts, until the table steward's question refocused my attention. He asked me, "Is there something that you would like to have that is not on the menu?"

I am not sure why, but I heard myself say, "Yes, black caviar!" I had not tasted caviar in years. Perhaps that is the reason why I ordered it. For the next sixteen days, before I could rebuttal, black caviar appeared on my plate. Never before had I experienced instantaneous service. I did not know how to tell the steward I had had enough of the gourmet, caviar appetizer.

Each night the same group of six new acquaintances sat together conversing casually and responding politely to all inquiries. At first we relayed superficial answers to all questions, until little by little, we revealed more and more details about ourselves. However after the first evening's dinner, I did not linger at the table and hurried off to attend a cabaret show. After the show, I walked around the ship, discovering several bar-lounges where different type of music was being played from classical to jazz. My favorite lounge was on the top Lido Deck, where an Italian band, the Rolandos, played a variety of dance music. While sitting at the bar to listen to the music, I ordered a rye and whiskey and lit up a Lucky Strike cigarette. A tap on my shoulder caused me to turn around, and I heard the cheerful greeting, "Hi, neighbor."

It was Cherie, the young lady I had met who had been sitting at the dinner table. She asked me if I could dance, and of course I said, "Yes!" We danced and chatted for the rest of the night. She explained that after graduating from college, she began working for her father's insurance company in Canada. Six months later, she decided to take a vacation, choosing this extravagant cruise, completely paid for by her father. For the next few days, she was my dancing partner. We enjoyed our time together, until the day she invited me to stay overnight in her cabin. I could not accept her flattering offer. I refused to become intimate with a girl who was nearly as young as my daughter. Looking for a more lasting relationship, I delicately, but honestly explained my feelings and suggested that we should not spoil our friendship and merely continue to be dancing partners. Surprised by my comments or not understanding my refusal, she made no comment and abruptly turned and walked away. Fortunately for both of us, Cherie had no trouble finding another male companion.

Wearing shorts and a button-down shirt on the second day of cruising, I stretched out on a chaise lounge absorbing the sun and enjoying the sea breezes. Unbuttoning and opening my shirt to the waste, I exposed part of my fair skinned chest. The next thing I remember is an attendant tapping me on the shoulder saying, "Sir, you should cover-up because you are sunburned." Sitting up, I could feel my skin stinging. Looking down at my chest, I saw the red sunburn in the shape of a triangle. No matter how many times I sat in the sun trying to even out my tan, the triangle shape was always darker. Since the ratio of females to males on this cruise for single adults was about six females to one male, it was not necessary to call attention to myself, but my unique sunburn became a funny conversation piece causing the passengers, mostly females, to comment, "You have the Bermuda Triangle tattooed on your chest."

When I attended dance lessons to learn the latest dance rage, the California Hustle, the majority of the participants were females. The lessons were held each morning at ten. An attractive lady stood next to me on the first day of the dance class. Not speaking, but smiling at one another, we concentrated on mastering the basic dance steps, as everyone stood in lines with the instructor in front. After the first session, I quickly departed, anxious to disembark at the first port of call, St. Thomas, Virgin Islands.

Joining Hans and Kurt on my first excursion to St. Thomas was a great idea, because Kurt was familiar with the attractions on the island. He was a plant manager for an electrical manufacturing company located in San Juan, Puerto Rico, and he would regularly indulge in weekend shuttle flights to St. Thomas. Because of his many visits and his familiarity with all aspects of the island, he was a natural tour guide. The three of us took a taxi from the dock, and our first stop was a restaurant next to Blue Beard's Castle to sample the world-famous drink, the banana daiquiri. Sitting at a sunken bar, our view overlooked St. Thomas harbor and Frenchman's Reef. The rocky terrain and white sandy beach leading to crystal clear, aqua-blue water was an island paradise. I felt like never leaving this fantastic island and could understand why Kurt returned often to St. Thomas. We ordered the drinks and Kurt warned me not to have more than one daiquiri. Because the deliciously smooth fruit-drink refreshed and cooled my dry throat, I swallowed the cocktail quickly. I ordered another one intending to drink it slowly, but the taxi driver announced that it was time for us to leave, so I gulped down the rest of the exotic beverage. When I stood-up, I immediately dropped to my knees. I was not drunk, but my legs did not support me. They were paralyzed! The brothers were laughing and reminded me of their warning not to have more than one. They helped me up and dragged me to the taxi for a return trip to the ship, where I rested and ate something to settle my stomach. I felt better, left the ship, and toured the shopping district on my own to purchase cases of liquor, because Kurt informed me of the availability of the inexpensive, duty-free alcohol. Every bottle of liquor was a bargain, especially the Napoleon cognac, smooth tasting rum called Bacalleta, and Canadian Club whiskey. The three cases of liquor that I had purchased were delivered to the ship and stored until the end of the cruise. The friendly merchants were willing to oblige other purchases, for I behaved like a typical tourist, buying all sorts of keepsakes for my family and me.

The following morning, I arrived on time for the "hustle" dance lesson on Lido Deck. The instructor's request to find a dance partner came easily, when I simply turned toward the same attractive lady who had stood next to me once again today. I held out my hand that joined naturally with my new partner, Francois, from Montreal, Canada. After the lesson, I invited her for a drink. We chatted, learning that we had a few things in common. We were the same age, recently divorced, had a daughter, and were interested in meeting new people. Working as an executive in one of the largest salt producing companies in Canada, Francois decided to take time off. She was traveling with a recently widowed girlfriend, who was a wealthy owner of a Canadian trucking company. Intrigued with one another, we managed to enjoy each other's company for the rest of the cruise. I had never been with another woman since marrying Renee, yet I was instantly comfortable with Francois. It was as if we had known each other for many years.

The second port of call was La Guaira, Venezuela, where Francois and I boarded a shuttle bus to Caracas, the capital, where we toured on foot. We saw the president of Venezuela, in a chauffer-driven white Ford Crown Victoria, the same make and color of the car I owned in the United States. His vehicle passed onto the driveway directly in front of us. I stepped closer to take a photo, but one of the guards standing near the entrance of the government building quickly blocked my shot and shouted, "No, photographs!" I merely wanted a picture of the Crown Victoria to show my family and friends the type of car the president used, but taking the photo was not allowed.

After that incident, we walked to the Simon Bolivar Museum dedicated to the famous South American general who was born in Caracas and fought for the country's independence from Spain. It was interesting to learn the history of the area, but we could not overstay for we had to return to our bus that would continue to the next destination, the Officers Casino, where we would be allotted time to gamble. Francois headed for the slot machines, but since I was a novice at gambling I merely strolled around the room choosing to observe rather than participate. Standing quietly behind the people seated at one of the roulette tables, I carefully watched how the game was played. I noticed that a player was given chips that were a different color from the other players seated at the table. Making a bet seemed easy for a player would place a chip or chips on the number, color, or sets he or she wanted to bet, while a small ball revolved around the roulette wheel. Then, the dealer waved his hand over the table signaling that no more bets were to be placed on the table. When the ball dropped into the winning slot, the dealer would announce the number and color, and then he would place a marker on the winning number. Scooping up all the losing bets or chips and making payouts in chips to the winners completed one round of a game.

Once a seat was available at one of the roulette tables, I confidently sat down and placed two one-hundred-dollar bills on the table, and the dealer gave me forty chips worth five dollars each. I placed one chip on red and another one on the line between numbers four and seven. Amazingly, number seven red came out, and I won chips. I continued betting randomly, winning often. After a while Francois approached telling me that it was time to leave, so I cashed in my pile of chips that totaled $2,230. Flabbergasted, I managed to declare, "I didn't realize I was a good gambler. From now on, my game is roulette at all the casinos!"

Santa Marta, Colombia, a gorgeous city with a natural harbor to the Caribbean Sea and magnificent mountain views, was the next port of call.

Before disembarking on our tour, the cruise director strongly recommended that no jewelry be worn because on several previous occasions passengers had been robbed. He explained that one lady's gold earring was pulled off her earlobe. Francois and I heeded his advice and boarded the tour bus wearing no jewelry, but excited to view this glorious city. The bus stopped at Santa Marta Cathedral, the first church constructed in Santa Marta, the oldest Spanish settlement. The Spanish were there in search of gold and jewels and neglected the valuable land and other resources.

We returned to the bus to continue our tour. About a mile from the next attraction, a luxurious casino-resort, the bus was forced to stop at a military roadblock, where a group of Colombian soldiers were stationed. Two of the soldiers boarded our bus and strolled down the aisle carefully scrutinizing each passenger. They did not speak. After their inspection, they exited, and the bus was permitted to continue on the road. At the entranceway of the resort, armed guards stopped the bus once again. The inspections and the ten-foot high, barbed-wire fence surrounding the facility were necessary to prevent the local criminals from entering. The resort, mostly frequented by tourists and obviously off limits to the poor inhabitants of Santa Marta who could not afford the high prices charged at this plush vacation facility, was like an oasis in the desert. The tourists wanted to have fun and mainly thought about their own gratifications. They rarely considered who benefited from the profits made from patronizing the lavish establishment. Francois and I did not care about the local politics or problems. We were like all the other tourists. Focusing on enjoying ourselves was our prime objective.

As soon as we left the bus, Francois and I headed for the beach. A replica of an old Spanish sailing ship was transformed into a bar-restaurant with ornate woodwork and sculptures. We ordered cocktails. Later, we ate lunch in the main hotel-restaurant. The employees seemed to be Colombians who could speak fluent English and treated us courteously. I especially enjoyed drinking the most flavorful coffee that was brewed with salty water.

Heading back to the cruise ship, the bus retraced the same route, stopping once again at the military checkpoint. Though this inspection of the soldiers did not surprise me, I felt uncomfortable, for their presence reminded me of wartime and military rule. I had become a complacent American citizen who took for granted the daily freedoms around me. When encountering this strange situation of extreme restrictions of freedom, I could not wait to be aboard the *Oceanic* again and sailing to Curaçao, away from the controlling environment.

When the *Oceanic* sailed on the high seas, the dress code for the passengers during dinnertime required formal attire. On the evening that the ship was heading for Curaçao, I started dressing for dinner and barely managed to button my trousers and jacket. Gaining weight was easy for me, since I have always loved food and partook of nearly all the seven meals provided daily. The schedule for food consumption began at six o'clock in the morning with an early-bird breakfast served continental style or at seven thirty, a full-served breakfast from a menu of scrumptious choices. More enticing food was served at ten o'clock that included soup with finger sandwiches. At noontime a tempting lunch was offered with a choice to eat at the poolside barbecue or at the dining room buffet. Then for those who wanted to snack again at three o'clock in the afternoon, tea or coffee with assorted pastries were available. A full course dinner was served each night at the early and late seatings. For those who were still hungry, a buffet, with any type of food desired from marinated tongue to strawberries dipped in chocolate, was picturesquely displayed at eleven o'clock at night. Then finally at three o'clock the next morning, pizza could be eaten at the bar lounges. Every food was exquisitely presented, so I could not resist sampling small morsels at first and then gluttonously consuming larger portions. No wonder I had gained twenty-four pounds at the end of the sixteen-day cruise!

After dinner that night, I had played roulette at the ship's casino and had lost five hundred dollars. I headed to the lounge on Lido Deck, where I could dance instead of losing any more money. Dancing was more fun anyway.

The next day, Francois and I shopped in Curacao, the largest island of the Netherlands, Antilles, where I purchased a new formal wardrobe. I also bought an outfit similar to clothes worn by a French sailor, including a black and white striped shirt, a black scarf for a belt, black pants, a sailor's cap, and a red bandana for my neck. Since the evening's festivities aboard the ship would be based on a Parisian theme, the French sailor's attire would be suitable for me to wear. Francois chose a more risqué outfit to complement mine. A mini-skirt, mesh stockings, a low-cut blouse, and a black beret made Francois look daring, yet not indecent. In fact her appearance suggested that she might be a French street walker. She looked very sexy.

After shopping, we felt at ease strolling among the friendly inhabitants who were as sweet as the liqueur we drank. My impression of Curacao was limited to the shopping excursions in the fancy stores and market place, yet this tropical island that was a colony of the Netherlands, was immaculately clean and refined. Returning to the ship came too soon for I wanted to spend more time exploring this tropical paradise.

The staff on board the *Oceanic* had worked diligently transforming the dining room into the city of Paris. A replica of the Eiffel Tower stood in the middle of the room, and a red, white, and blue striped French flag adorned the flowered centerpiece at each table. The waiters, wearing white aprons, red kerchiefs tied around their necks, and blue berets tilted to one side of their heads, handed us menus describing only French cuisine. The finale was the dessert, baked Alaska flambé, served with the most delicious French brandy as an after dinner cordial.

Positive and flattering comments were made about my choice of being a French sailor. Perhaps, the Picart influence was filtering through my costumed appearance, for part of my heritage could be traced to the southwestern part of France. I believed that my love for boating and being on the high seas also qualified me to be a sailor. My companion, a French-Canadian, Francois spoke both French and English fluently. With her encouragement, I began speaking simple phrases and sentences in French. Understanding was easier, but relearning the pronunciation was more difficult. Gradually, I began to embrace my French heritage for the first time in my life, a feeling that never surfaced when I was in the French Foreign Legion. It felt as if Grandfather Jon Pierre Picart was surely smiling down on me, approving my behavior.

The evening's entertainment also followed a Parisian theme with the master of ceremonies introducing the talented females, performing the famous French dance, the can-can. This outrageous dance was originally introduced in the Paris dance halls in the late nineteenth century. Romance was in the air, as Francois and I danced the night away into the wee hours of the morning.

Aruba was my favorite port of call. Francois and I toured the northeast side of the island to view the famous Natural Coral Bridge. Our guide explained that this natural bridge was formed through erosion from the sea, carving a one-hundred-foot bridge that extended twenty-five feet over the sea. Interestingly, he continued to explain that on every second day, dumpsters would spill food waste from the bridge into the water, causing a feeding frenzy, for hungry fish and for the sharks that would devour the food and fish as well. I can see why the natives call the bridge "the ugly mouth." Family members who visited Aruba in 2006 informed me that this natural phenomenon no longer exists.

Our tour continued to Fort Zoulman, Oranjestad, which houses the Aruba Historical Museum, and most impressive were the divi-divi trees because their trunks grow straight and the branches and leaves grow southward. I think that the divi-divi trees were shaped like an upside-down letter L and looked most unusual. I was fascinated to learn that Aruba is outside the hurricane belt with pleasant weather all the time from cooling trade winds resulting in little rainfall and no humidity. Our guide mentioned that most of the resorts on the island guaranteed perfect weather, and if it ever did rain all day, vacation time would be extended an extra day.

After touring the spots of interests, we spent the rest of the time purchasing clothes in the many shops in Aruba. I had to buy another suitcase to hold the additional purchases made during the trip. Hating to leave Aruba, we reluctantly returned to the ship, for if we had missed the sailing, we would have had to use our own funds and means of transportation to get to the next port of call. It was tempting to stay behind on this lovely island.

After dinner that evening, the cruise director reminded the passengers about the next day's schedule of events, in particular, the masquerade ball. Racks of costumes would be available at one of the lounges, and a selection of a favorite costume to wear could be made by anyone wanting to participate. Francois and I decided to take part in the masquerade ball, so we tried on costumes. Since I had gained weight, many of my selections did not fit properly. I nearly gave up, but then I noticed a Roman toga that was loose fitting and could be wrapped around my body. I found a laurel wreath to encircle my head. It was ideal. I would proclaim to be Julius Caesar, emperor of Rome. Francois found a perfect complement to my costume. She would be Cleopatra!

The next evening after dinner, we returned to our rooms and changed into our masquerade costumes. We emerged as Caesar and Cleopatra. Along with more than fifty other couples, we entered a contest for the best costumes worn by a couple. A total of nine judges, members of the staff, a few officers, and four passengers, would rate our appearance as we paraded around. When it was time and Francois and I were called, I lifted my right arm, as she rested her left hand palm down on top of my extended hand. Acting the role of our characters as if in a play, we walked regally around the room pausing in front of the judges. We managed not to laugh and maintained our personas with dignity and poise until the very end. After the final couple was judged, the cruise director announced the winners starting with third place. Competing with the intension of pure merriment, we had not expected to win, so when the cruise director announced, "The first place winners are Caesar and Cleopatra!" we were astonished. I was presented with a silver pen, and Francois received a silver bracelet. Both prizes were inscribed with the name of our cruise ship, *Oceanic*. From that day on, most of the passengers and crew called us Caesar and Cleopatra. A smile forms on my lips when I think of the fun time impersonating Caesar "and the glory that was cruising on the *Oceanic*."

The very last port of call before sailing back to New York harbor was the Bahamas, West Indies, noted for numerous straw markets and shops selling everything from shark's teeth to expensive jewelry. Whether driving or walking, whoever crosses the bridge from Freeport to Paradise Island must pay one dollar to visit the most famous attraction, the Casino on Paradise Island. Anxious to try my hand at gambling, once again I joined other players at the roulette table. Picking the winning spins seemed impossible for me that day. Gambling resulted in a devastating loss of all the money I had won at the other casinos including the extra money I had set aside. I concluded that I loved to play roulette, but I did not like losing, so gambling was not for me.

As I was about to retreat from my roulette seat, I turned in the direction of loud voices oooohing and ahhhhhhing. The arrival of an entourage with Stavros Niarchos, the Greek shipping magnate and the former brother-in-law of Aristotle Onassis, caused a commotion. He and his associates were escorted to a private roulette table, immediately surrounded by guards blocking anyone from approaching. As I left the casino, chatter about the Greek tycoon's arrival escalated. Even my cab driver pointed out the huge, silver yacht belonging to Niarchos that was docked securely at the pier. I thought to myself, "How much is he going to lose at roulette?" I had learned the lesson that there are no sure winners in any type of gambling.

A newsletter about world events was delivered to each cabin daily. Whenever I retrieved the paper that I found tucked under my cabin door, it was deposited into the wastebasket for I had no desire reading about the news anywhere around the world. The *Oceanic* had become my world. When the day arrived for our farewell dinner, I did not want to leave the ship for I adored my fantasy world. Francois seemed to love being apart of my new world. We lingered that last night and partied along with other passengers. It seemed that none of us wanted this fabulous cruise to end. My mood soon turned as gloomy as the cold, rainy, ugly day in New York harbor. The only bright side was that Francois and I had planned to see one another after the cruise, and we did.

Back home meant back to reality. Returning to work and not using the remainder of the time I had requested for a leave-of-absence was a good decision; yet cruising was a way to do something just for me, rejuvenating my life. When the personnel manager reminded me that I still had three weeks left of vacation time, I booked my second cruise, a seven-day trip to Bermuda on the *Statendam* for the first week in June. For me cruising again was not an impulsive decision, but a firm commitment to know myself in different settings and to tour beautiful places. I was ready to be on the move with my life.

Francois and I kept our promise to see one another, even though we lived far apart. She suggested that I visit for a weekend, and I readily accepted her invitation, looking forward to being with her again. Leaving New Jersey early in the morning and driving about eight hours, I reached Montreal by Saturday evening. I should have been tired, but I was energized and genuinely happy when Francois and I greeted one another. We embraced and chatted like two teenagers, catching up on the latest gossip. It was nice to be with someone who cared. Francois showed me around her luxuriously decorated penthouse apartment. It was a magnificent dwelling, yet Francois made me feel comfortable in her plush surroundings. She had made plans to dine at an exclusive restaurant in the Bonaventure Hotel. After I freshened up and changed my clothes, we drove to the restaurant about two blocks away. As soon as we entered the establishment, the maitre d' greeted Francois by name and seated us at a booth. With a lovely companion at my side, the champagne toast, and scrumptious food were added bonuses. I asked the waiter for the check, but Francois explained that the bill had already been taken care of and added to her tab. Her generosity was appreciated, but I felt somewhat uncomfortable about her paying.

Sunday morning, we went to breakfast at a restaurant located in the part of the city known as Old Montreal. The atmosphere was elegant with the décor resembling furnishings from the Victorian era. A string ensemble played chamber music. I wanted to linger, but I knew that the drive back to New Jersey would be a long one. Even though the Northern Highway from Montreal to Albany, New York, was one of the most scenic routes, my experience driving on it was not a good one. Driving alone for a long distance, especially when sleepy, was not easy. Even with the radio blasting, I seemed to still have trouble staying awake. I smoked two packs of cigarettes. It was a terrible drive!

When planning my next visit to see Francois, I made up my mind to fly instead of driving. I flew from La Guardia Airport in New York to

Montreal on Thursday afternoon and returned Sunday evening. My stay was more relaxing and less stressful, and allotted more time for Francois and me to visit with Ruth, her girlfriend from the cruise. We were invited to lunch at Ruth's elaborate house on the outskirts of Montreal. Her maid served us impeccably.

That evening, I insisted on treating them to dinner, and they selected a Greek restaurant, one of their favorite eateries. This time the maitre d' greeted them both by name. As we were escorted to our table, the girls stopped to chat with a couple at another table. I was introduced as an acquaintance from New Jersey, and I simply smiled and nodded. Once seated at our table, I looked around approving the Grecian ambience with picturesque statues placed between white columns and large paintings of Athens and Acropolis adorning the walls. Depicting the Greek cultural heritage, each waiter was dressed in authentic Greek clothes. The outfit consisted of a black hat with a tassel; a white, puffed long-sleeved shirt; an ornate black, bolero jacket; a white knee-high skirt; a white leotard covering for the legs; and black shoes. While listening to Greek music, we consumed all sorts of Greek specialties, including imported wines and ouzo, an after dinner cordial. Once their services to the customers were completed, the waiters became entertainers performing the Greek line dance, waving a white handkerchief and eventually breaking plates on the tiled floors. We laughed and agreed that breaking dishes was one way to avoid washing them.

Francois planned sightseeing tours to Mt. Montreal and more reservations at fancy restaurants. I was enjoying this glamorous relationship of living the high society lifestyle.

Two weeks later, Francois flew to Teterboro Airport in New Jersey on her corporate jet to attend a conference in New York City. After her business appointment, we met at my apartment, and I took her to dinner at the Fisherman's Restaurant in Saddle Brook. It was not as remarkable as the restaurants we patronized in Montreal, but Francois did not mind. This sophisticated lady's down-to-earth manner was most attractive to me.

Francois and I were growing closer and fonder of one another, so much so, that she suggested that I move in with her. She offered me a job with her company in my line of work as a quality control inspector. I was flattered at first, but after thinking carefully, I determined that I did not want to move away from the United States and my beloved family. I also considered the fact that I needed three more years of employment at the Ford plant before I could qualify for a pension, that I did not want to lose, and most important, I disliked the idea of being completely dependent on decisions made by Francois. I would be subordinate to her discretions. Her offer was not acceptable for me, yet tempting. If circumstances were different, I may have considered the move because Francois was a charming, intelligent, and beautiful lady.

I made one last trip to Montreal, explaining my decision in person. Francois was upset, but understood, and our parting was friendly but sad. We communicated for a while, with phone calls and letters, but I gradually stopped all communications for there was no reason to pursue our relationship. I could not just be a friend.

On a Sunday in May, I accepted Kurt's invitation to visit him, and I knew I would be playing ping-pong, because Kurt had challenged me to many games throughout the cruise. Our games were always friendly matches, but I surmised that Kurt was as competitive as I was and disliked losing. We both enjoyed the rivalry. Since I had the good fortune of winning more games, he mentioned playing ping-pong at his home where he felt that on his turf he could do much better. I also knew we would be conversing in German because Kurt preferred speaking German to those who knew the language to keep up his fluency. He and his brother Hans always spoke German together. Since they did not often see one another, Kurt would practice speaking with other acquaintances. When he asked me to converse in German, I obliged.

Arriving early Sunday morning, I stopped and spoke to the guard requesting my entry to an exclusive, gated community. Kurt resided in a luxurious house overlooking Candlewood Lake, a man-made lake in Connecticut. Creating a picturesque scene of tranquil beauty, a sailboat and a motorboat were secured to his private dock. A custom-built gazebo on the end of the dock provided a perfect spot to sit and gaze at the scenic view.

Kurt took me for a ride around the lake in the motorboat.

Inside Kurt's house, the furnishings and décor were elegantly expensive and comfortably practical. Deep-sea fishing was another avid sport, and telling notorious "fish stories" seemed to be a natural by-product, but a huge stuffed swordfish, a prized catch, did hang in the den. Since it was the housekeeper's day off, I was impressed when he made lunch and served it on the gazebo. After lunch we headed for the game room that included a ping-pong table as well as a pool table. We played ping-pong for a few hours. I cannot remember who won the most games, but I vividly recall our conversation about cruising. Since retiring, Kurt's new interest was traveling, booking two-to-three cruises a year. Since his girlfriend had a full time job, she could not accompany him, so he wanted me to join him on his next scheduled trip that would be taking him around the world. I told him that financially it would not be possible and emphasized that I had to return to work. Promising to meet again for a day of ping-pong, our schedules clashed and future visits did not materialize.

Meeting and forming brief friendships with Francois, Kurt, and other individuals on my cruise was not a waste of time for me. Relationships may not always develop into serious or more lasting friendships, but they are still important. I have read that some friends can be a part of your life for merely a season; yet their friendship may have a meaningful purpose. Francois and Kurt did not realize that they had helped me to figure out the path I should take in my life. My decision to stay in the United States helped me to learn more about myself. I was looking forward to meeting more individuals, encountering new situations, and making decisions that would continue to enrich my life.

My next adventure was a week in June of 1978 in balmy and beautiful Bermuda. I did not realize that my cruise to Bermuda would coincide with the silver jubilee anniversary celebration of the coronation of Queen Elizabeth II of Great Britain. I was in for wonderful surprises. The cruise ship, the *Statendam*, was docked on Front Street in Hamilton, Bermuda. It was an exceptional location to witness a four-day celebration on the island. Starting with a parade of boats in the harbor, the vessels, that seemed to include every watercraft from the island, were colorfully decorated with all sorts of flags and banners. The smallest boats to the largest yachts participated in the parade that lasted for several hours.

One evening, two bands; the Black Watch Royal Regiment and the Bermuda Regiment, with members in full-dressed uniforms, marched down Front Street. Passengers lined the decks, as if they were on a reviewing stand, to photograph the festivities. Cannons fired salutes and fireworks dazzled the spectators. After the parade, several high-ranking officers from the band regiments accepted the cruise captain's invitation to attend a cocktail party in honor of the queen. The passengers greeted them warmly, bestowing congratulations on their excellent performances.

Renting a moped for four days, a popular means of transportation, I parked it on the dock near the ship's entranceway. On my first day's excursion, I merrily drove toward the other side of the island, naturally driving on the right side as we do in the United States. When I turned the corner, the cars were heading directly at me. I quickly turned the moped onto the sidewalk, narrowly avoiding a major accident. Calming down after a few minutes, I realized I had forgotten that the traffic rules are different in Bermuda, requiring vehicles to drive on the left side of the road, as they do in England. From then on, I drove slowly and carefully. I followed the line of traffic, but it was hard to adjust to driving on the left side of the road; yet I would not give up the convenience of touring the island freely and independently. I would return to the ship only for the scheduled dinnertime.

The mild, sunny weather was always conducive for sightseeing. My favorite stops were at the pink, soft, sandy beaches, in particular Elbow Beach and Horseshoe Beach. Swimming in the crystal clear water was refreshingly delightful, and usually followed by a sweet, yet tangy, tropical drink, a typical daily treat. An excursion on a glass-bottom boat for observations of the underwater life around the island was another highlight. Coral reefs in various shapes and forms that could be vibrant or muted colors of red, orange, yellow, and pink were like tangled highways for the numerous fish swimming in and out and all around. A World War II destroyer was submerged in the water, with only the bow protruding over the surface. According to the tour guide, a German submarine had sunk the destroyer. It looked like an ugly scar and an unexpected distraction from the surrounding beauty.

Throughout Bermuda, businessmen were dressed in jackets and ties and Bermuda shorts and knee-high socks. Their style of dress looked both casual, yet distinguished in appearance. Another tour guide pointed out the villas on the island that were owned by Henry Ford and Nelson Rockefeller, wealthy and famous Americans. I was beginning to feel like a rich American on vacation, adapting quickly to life of leisure. I was, once again, free from worries and responsibilities.

After four glorious days on the British-controlled island of Bermuda, the *Statendam* departed in the evening, heading home to the port of New York. The next morning, stormy weather with strong winds and torrential rains caused twenty-foot waves to crash over the stern. The rough waters and violent weather continued all day, causing the captain to announce that the decks would be secured with no passengers permitted outside. When the gale storm worsened, the ship began pitching more severely, and most of the passengers were seasick. At dinnertime, the tables were about half empty, and at show time, more passengers and several entertainers were noticeably missing at the performance. I was among the minority who did not suffer from seasickness. I continued to eat, drink, and dance until one by one the last of the musicians disappeared.

The following morning, the *Statendam* docked safely, but the day was gloomy and cloudy, reflecting my mood, for I did not want to disembark. Leaving my pampered existence was like a king being evicted from his castle, but my melancholy did not last, for I felt refreshed and renewed. I walked briskly down the runway to the awaiting car service ready to move forward with my life.

A daily routine of working at the Ford Mahwah Plant consumed most of my time, but I also had time to pal around with the same group of friends. Ray, my supervisor, and Frank, a general foreman, not only worked with me, but also were my buddies and neighbors when I had resided in Paramus. We still remained good friends. A member of the Benevolent and Protective Order of Elks in Paramus, Ray would casually mention the fun activities he and his wife attended at the Elks Lodge. Joining Ray and his wife at a Saturday night dinner-dance was my initial introduction into Elkdom. I questioned Ray further about the Elks and learned that the organization was a charitable order dedicated to the welfare of veterans and youth, especially handicapped children. Awarding scholarships to further educational goals, sponsoring drug awareness and prevention activities, promoting other programs to benefit the needy in the community were completed by the impressive Elks. I told Ray that I would consider joining.

I did not only socialize with co-workers, but also former acquaintances from the Paramus Police Reserves who would keep in touch, in particular two dear friends, Richard and Mary. They would often invite me to their home for dinner. On one of these occasions, they introduced me to Terri, their neighbor who was newly divorced. Terri had custody of her four children, two girls and two boys, ranging in age from twelve years old to the older son who was in the army. Whenever there was a dance at the Elks, Terri would be my date and dancing partner. We got along and dated seriously.

A few months later, I asked Terri to join me on my third cruise that was going to the eastern Caribbean. Not able to get off from work or leave her children, she regretfully declined my offer, but I decided to cruise again anyway. The *Rotterdam* left the port of New York, stopping at St. Thomas, St. John, Barbados, and Bahamas. I had no trouble meeting ladies on the cruise, but they were not special or lasting relationships. For the first time after visiting glorious places, I was anxious to return home. Cruising was wonderful, but once the fun filled, carefree vacation was over, I did not feel any better or completely satisfied. I admitted to myself that cruising through life was not the answer, and I needed a life with more practical goals.

The choices made in the next year directed me on the true path to a new life. Ray sponsored me as a member of the Paramus Elks Lodge #2001, and I was officially initiated in November of 1978. Andy, John, and Steve, friends and fellow co-workers at the Ford plant, would also attend the bi-monthly meetings with Ray and me. In fact, John and Tony knew me well when I was their chief of the Paramus Police Reserves and a fellow member of the Paramus Pistol League.

My attendance at each Elks' meeting not only enabled me to socialize with friends, but also increased my awareness of the responsibilities of the officers, the committees, and the entire Elks' structure. At first, I was comfortable attending the meetings as a member in good standing, but then at one of these meetings, John nominated me for a position on the board of trustees for five years, and Steve seconded his nomination. I almost declined, but Andy and Ray encouraged me to accept. Since two other members were running for the same position and no other members present knew me well, except my four friends, I thought I could not possibly win. Surprisingly, I had the most votes and was installed as a Five-Year Trustee in April of 1979. Required to wear a tuxedo at each meeting and special functions, I put my two tuxedos to good use. Terri and I continued dating and attended many Elks' events. I was having fun, while contributing to benevolent accomplishments. Joining the Paramus Elks was one of the best decisions in my life.

While living in Saddle Brook, I ran into Wayne Wichart, an acquaintance from the Bergen County Police Reserve Pistol League and a lieutenant on the Saddle Brook Police Specials. When Wayne found out I lived in town, he said, "The Saddle Brook Police Reserves could use a man with your experience. Why don't you join us?"

I eagerly responded, "Yes, I will join!" I became the Pistol Range Officer in charge of training new reservists in the safe use of guns during Saturday target practices and weekly league competitions. Patrol assignments and a detail as a bailiff on court nights were additional duties that I thoroughly enjoyed. My involvement with the Paramus Elks and the Saddle Brook Police Reserves kept me busy. Meeting many interesting people was an added bonus. My life was taking on a new direction, with lots of stimulating activities for my mind and body.

Attending my first New Jersey State Elks Convention in Wildwood, I volunteered to carry the American flag for the Paramus lodge, with an Elk member marching on each side of me as guards. After the parade, I discussed with Walter Pauselius, the new Exalted Ruler, the possibility of establishing a formal color guard for our lodge. I declared my willingness to head the project and emphasized my past experiences as the captain of the color guard for the Elmwood Park Fire Department and the Paramus Police Reserves. He granted permission and the Paramus Elks Color Guard was started. Seven members volunteered: one to carry the American flag, another to carry the New Jersey state flag, a third to carry the Elks flag, and four members to carry rifles. As the captain, I would carry a saber that was one of the many weapons from my brother Alex's collection. He kindly allowed me to keep the saber. It was from the American Revolution with the engraved words, U.S. Cavalry Captain Company C. The saber is a gift I will always cherish.

Most of the volunteer Elks for the color guard were former military men who already knew the fundamentals of marching, making my job easier. We drilled as often as we could, presenting arms and practicing different formations and movements. The color guard was ready to lead the Paramus lodge's contingent at the next New Jersey State Elks Convention Parade. Wearing the same outfits as the marching membership: black pants, white short-sleeved shirt, and a black cowboy hat, the Paramus Elks Color Guard won the first place award out of one hundred thrity-nine lodges. This first win was one of many proud moments that extended over my twenty years as the captain of the color guard.

Every year the color guard competition at the New Jersey State Convention became more competitive, yet the Paramus Elks Color Guard managed a first, second, or third place award. Though we wore many outfits, a favorite one was my design of a white, purple, and gold uniform. It was similar in style to the uniforms worn by the cadets at the West Point Military Academy. Dressed impeccably, the members of the color guard would march in a triangle-shaped formation with me carrying the saber in front. Forming the second row, three men marched directly behind me. The tallest man carried the American flag, flanked by a rifleman on each side. The third row consisted of four men. One man carried the New Jersey state flag and marched next to another man who carried the Elks flag. A rifleman flanked each flag-carrying Elk. This eight-man color guard was made up of various members through out the years. Alex joined the group for several years, alternating as a flag or rifle carrier. Though my marching days are over, the Paramus Elks Color Guard has continued to maintain a high standard of performance, obtaining awards and accolades throughout the state of New Jersey. I am proud to have been the initiator of its existence.

Another interesting time in my life that may also be considered a turning point occurred on June 29, 1980. This was the day when the largest Ford Motor Assembly Plant built in Mahwah, New Jersey, ceased operations. Twenty-five years of non-stop production of cars and trucks in the Mahwah plant was over. The shortages and high prices of gasoline during the late 1970s caused sales to plummet and was one of the reasons for the closing. Other reasons involved labor problems. My brother and I were fortunate to be offered an early retirement or a transfer to San Jose, California; Detroit, Michigan; or Kansas City, Kansas. We both chose early retirement, for we did not want to relocate, leaving family and friends. My son Mike, not having accumulated enough years to vest his pension, left the Ford plant to become an electrical apprentice. He maintained an electrician's license and eventually advanced as a foreman.

Employed at the Ford Mahwah Plant until the end of July, I was one of the last workers to leave, overseeing the proper crating and shipping of the quality control instruments from my department to other Ford factories. To dismantle and scrap the car parts was decided by management to be more cost effective instead of transporting the material to other facilities. Completing these tasks took several weeks, and finally after twenty-five years and two months, my employment at the Ford plant had ended. Leaving a secure job was sad, but Ford failing was sadder. Ford failing was like America failing. It seemed un-American to think in negative terms, but at fifty-three years of age I was not certain which direction to follow. Heeding the positive lessons prescribed and modeled by my parents, I became energized to move on and start again. Thankfully, Ford had not abandoned me, for the company continued paying my salary for a year, while I pondered over the dilemma of what to do after that.

I learned about a retraining program for former Ford employees. Ford and the United States government would provide a special grant with combined funding. Some of my fellow employees did not take advantage of further retraining and missed out on the limited time offer. I decided to apply, so in September of 1980, I attended classes at Bergen County Technical Institute in Hackensack for two semesters in the field of quality control, my expertise. The courses emphasized the reading of advanced engineering blueprints that detailed various manufacturing parts from medical instruments to airplane parts.

After completing a year of study, the school recommended a job at Advanced Technology Systems, a division of Austin Methods, in Fair Lawn as a quality control inspector. My job was to inspect any incoming mechanical or electrical components that were used for different jobs. The parts for a flight simulator, a submarine periscope, night vision, lasers, and computerized fire controls for ships were inspected according to the blueprints and military specifications. Readily adjusting to the new job and fellow workers, I was happy in my new position. Change is good! At first I was fearful of change, but once I committed positive efforts, a successful transition evolved. I am grateful to the Ford Motor Company for providing the initial means for my success. Both Ford and I survived. It was worth cheering!

Forming a friendship with Chris, the purchasing agent at Advanced Technology Systems, who was also a member of the Saddle Brook Police Reserves, was a pleasant surprise. Into my second year of employment, my knowledge of the use of firearms proved to be an interesting asset to finalize the company's project, Night Fighter, or night vision. The newly developed Night Fighter consisted of synchronized goggles with a tube that projected an infrared dot and enabled the person wearing the goggles to see objects in almost complete darkness. The objects would be seen as a silhouette, green in color. The pulsating dot of light, visible only to the person wearing the goggles, would project from the cylinder that could be aimed at the targeted object in view. The company's goal was to fasten the cylinder to a pistol or rifle, because the Night Fighter was earmarked for police, combat troops, and security personnel. At a company meeting to discuss the solutions for the problem of mounting the night vision tube to a gun, Chris happened to mention my name and expertise with guns. The manager asked for my assistance and after evaluating the problem, I suggested that a bracket could be made to secure the cylinder to the firearm. I also commented that my brother Alex could possibly design one.

Alex had also taken advantage of the retraining program after retiring from his job at the Ford plant. His training resulted in employment as a gunsmith, not only a career, but also his hobby and passion. He was employed as a supervisor at Navy Arms in Union City. The company manufactured replicas of authentic firearms and refurbished and repaired guns and rifles from every era. Most of the firearms produced by the company were custom made. I was sure that Alex could design a bracket for the night vision to fit any type of gun. After meeting the managerial staff at Advanced Technology Systems and discussing the problem, Alex easily created an aluminum bracket that secured the cylinder to a Colt .45 caliber handgun. His services were free of charge. My little brother was doing me a favor.

To determine if Alex's design would work, I obtained permission from the Saddle Brook police chief to test the new Night Fighter gun at the Saddle Brook Pistol Range. The engineers from Advanced Technology Systems, the police chief, two police officers, and Alex watched my demonstration. The range lights were turned off and the target was in darkness. Wearing the goggles, my view of the target was green, yet visible. The sight on the gun was synchronized with the goggles and the cylinder. Wherever I aimed the dotted light, the bullet would hit the dotted spot. I shot the bull's eye on an L-target from twenty-five yards without going out of the nine-ring. Everyone was astounded, including me, with the accuracy of my shooting. It was easier than shooting in the daylight. Alex's bracket design had worked! Once the managers of the company realized the successful outcome of the bracket on the gun, they requested the mounting of another bracket on an M-16 Night Fighter rifle. Alex obliged!

Advanced Technology Systems was ready to market the night vision products. I was called upon to demonstrate the Night Fighter on several occasions. My last demonstration was at the National Rifle Range in Cherry Hill, New Jersey, for the military. Four high-ranking army officers observed as I shot at a target one hundred meters away with a rifle. Shooting confidently and hitting the center of an L-target, my accuracy was a marvel, however, the officers were skeptical and wanted to see me shoot again. The lights were turned off and before starting to shoot, I noticed a rabbit sitting about fifty meters away. I mentioned to the officer who was standing on my left, "I see a rabbit down range. I am going to take him out." The officer made no comment.

After shooting, the spotlights were turned on to reveal a perfect target score and a dead rabbit. The only response from the army officers was, "Unbelievable!" They thanked me and left. The next morning, I learned that my shooting demonstrations would no longer be needed since the American military had acquired the night vision product. It always makes me proud to think that Alex and I played a small part in the development of night vision on firearms. My only response, "Unbelievable!"

In 1983, the entire Austin Methods division in New Jersey had been consolidated with the main headquarters in Cleveland, Ohio. Presented with options to move, of course, my answer was to refuse. Within a week, I had another job as a quality control inspector for Phillips Precision, a company that manufactured surgical tools. My friend, Chris, decided not to relocate to Ohio either and was hired by Lucas Aerospace Company in Fairfield, New Jersey. Even though we no longer worked for the same company, we would see one another at police reserve activities.

About two years later, Chris informed me of an opening at Lucas in the inspection field. I was excited about applying for this more challenging position. The company's newest project was the creation of the fuel control system for the V-22 Osprey airplane. In addition to research and development, other projects consisted of overhauling the starter engines, hydraulic systems, and electronic components for the Harrier V-8 Fighter. Updating and submitting my resume, I felt that this was my chance to work in the aviation field, one of my longtime desires.

I was one of ten applicants being interviewed at Lucas. At fifty-eight years of age, I was also the oldest interviewee, and the only man without a college degree. Three engineers and the quality control manager questioned me for an hour about my technical knowledge and experiences, as well as my personal history. After I had deciphered several blueprints with accuracy, their final question was, "If you were accepted to fill the position, would you be able to travel throughout the United States and at times to England to complete source inspections at various companies that manufacture components for Lucas?"

My answer was, "If you give me time to go home and pack, I would travel anytime and anywhere." Smiles formed on their faces and on my face, too.

Two weeks later, I received a letter of congratulations on my selection as a quality control inspector at Lucas Aerospace Company, beginning on April 1, 1985. When I read the date, I was leery and thought it might be an April Fool's Day trick, but after phoning to confirm my acceptance, my boss Hal assured me that the date was correct.

I worked for one year as the inspector for incoming components shipped to the company and used for projects. When I was promoted to a quality assurance representative, I began traveling on source inspections. Inspecting incoming components or traveling to inspect specified parts made at far away factories required the same procedures. First, I would review the paperwork, recording the materials used to make the part. If the materials satisfied the requirements, I would continue more detailed inspections, choosing several samples randomly to inspect, measuring, weighing or testing in a specific manor for the objects being inspected. If all items were acceptable, I would affix my official stamp to approve delivery, a decision I would take seriously.

On a few occasions, I would reject items that did not comply with the company's standards or military specifications. Accuracy in all inspections was critical to the development of a reliable product. I would never jeopardize my reputation or the company that entrusted me with this important job.

Most of my traveling experiences were pleasant, especially since the company paid for membership in the VIP lounges at the airports, entitling me to wait in a luxurious lounge with comfortable chairs, desks, tables, telephones, and televisions. Complimentary beverages were also available, while my boarding pass and luggage were processed.

An attendant would notify me when the plane was ready for passengers to board. Gradually my flight mileage accumulated, permitting me to upgrade my personal vacation flights.

During one of my trips to Washington state in November, my plane landed on Sunday afternoon at the Tacoma/Seattle airport, where I rented a car and drove to the nearby Holiday Inn. The next morning, I planned to drive to Bothell about thirty miles north of Seattle to a factory for a source inspection. Unexpectedly, an overnight snowfall, instead of the usual rain, caused several inches of accumulation on the ground. My trip to Bothell was still on schedule when I phoned and was informed that the plant would be open for business.

Not properly dressed or prepared for snowy conditions, I reluctantly trekked through the deep snow trying to find the new Volvo 640 four-door sedan in the hotel parking lot. All the vehicles were completely covered with snow. Finding the mound of snow with the Volvo beneath, I realized I needed something better than my bare hands to scrape the snow off the car. Returning to the hotel, I obtained a piece of cardboard. There was nothing else available. No one was ready for the large amount of snowfall.

After clearing the snow, I started off on my journey to Bothell. Once out of the city limits of Seattle on Route 5, I turned onto highway 522 that was banked on the turns like a racetrack. Because the road was not plowed and the below-freezing temperature caused the snow to harden and turn to ice, the traffic slowed. Most of the vehicles including mine started sliding down sideways, stopping eventually on the shoulder of the road that was level. Once a car slid to the shoulder of the road, it was trapped because the surface was too slippery and slanted to get back onto the highway. Coincidentally, a tow truck, secure with chains on its tires, pulled in front of my car. The truck driver offered a tow back onto the roadway for five dollars. I had to be towed four more times until reaching a level stretch of road that guided me directly to my destination. The driver of the tow truck must have made a bundle of money for nearly everyone needed his services. After being on the road for a few hours, I arrived safely, but the plant was closed. Traveling back to the hotel, I encountered no problems, but I was forced to stay another day.

A cell phone would have come in handy preventing my wasted trip, but there was no such device available for me at that time.

Another traveling fiasco occurred on a trip to California. When I arrived in Los Angeles at ten o'clock at night, I rented a car at the airport and drove northwest on Route 405 toward my hotel located in Van Nuys. About half way to the hotel and somewhere near Santa Monica, the car developed mechanical problems. Moving to the slow lane, the lights and engine quit functioning. I was able to safely roll onto the shoulder. I could see nothing, but darkness. Finding the flashlight in my briefcase, I used it to guide my way to the emergency phone alongside the highway. I phoned the rental company at the airport, telling them my location and the exact number posted on the emergency phone. Walking back to the car, I waited for an hour. Becoming impatient, I walked back to phone the rental company again and was told that only one tow truck was available and would arrive as soon as possible. I had no choice but to wait patiently. I waited and waited until two o'clock in the morning, when I was finally towed back to the rental office. I was fuming mad. My irate anger focused on the manager who repeatedly apologized and as a consolatory gesture, gave me a new Ford Crown Victoria to use free of charge. I arrived on time for the source inspection at nine in the morning, but I was tired! Having a cell phone would not have helped in this situation.

The following year, the Lucas Fairfield Division where I was employed dissolved the research department, causing a consolidation of employees and relocation to other divisions. Some employees were transferred to England and other parts of the United States. I was sent to Englewood, New Jersey, where mostly repair and overhaul of parts for the Airbus airplane and Harrier fighter were completed. Hal, my boss, retired, and Ray became my new superior. My job description stayed the same, source inspections.

In February of 1994, I traveled to Miami, Florida, with a female contract agent, Phyllis, for an inspection of precision gears. We completed our work and were ready to fly back to New Jersey on Thursday, but all the airports in the Northeast were closed because of a severe snowstorm. We could not return until Monday. Phyllis visited a cousin who lived nearby, while I toured attractions from Miami Beach to Key Biscayne.

My favorite spot was the American Federation of Police Museum, of which I am a charter member. As soon as I showed my membership card, I was given preferential treatment, a personal tour by a Miami police lieutenant, who was honored to meet a charter member. All sorts of police memorabilia were on display. I located the shoulder patches from the police and reservists from Paramus, New Jersey. The lieutenant also drove me to the Miami police headquarters and surrounding area. His tour was quite a treat.

Working for Lucas Aerospace had become a solid part of my life, and my involvement with the Paramus Elks and Saddle Brook Police Reserves consumed my free time. Terri and I continued dating until 1984, but simply stated, both of us could not agree to a future commitment. We parted amicably.

Cupid's arrow may not have been aimed in my direction, but happily pierced the heart of my son, Mike, who met and fell in love with a beautiful girl named Lori from Elmwood Park. They were married on May 12, 1984, a gloriously sunny spring day. The ceremony took place outside in a little park near Spring Valley Road in Paramus, and the reception for almost three hundred guests followed at the Paramus Elks Lodge. Since we both came without dates, Renee, my ex-wife and I were partners for the occasion. Everyone, including me, enjoyed the excitement of the wedding festivities. I especially recall observing the young, vibrant love between Mike and Lori and the older, familiar love between my Pop and Mom. It was heartwarming to compare the new and old. Both couples were elegantly dressed and dancing together at the wedding, and most evident was the loving devotion shining brightly for each pair of lovers. My parents' everlasting love, an inspiration for not only Mike and Lori, but for all of us, was a joy to behold. Hopefully, someday, I would find such a love.

At first the newlyweds rented a house on a large piece of property on the corner of Forest Avenue and Oradell Avenue in Paramus. They eventually purchased the house, subdivided the property, and on the empty lot, started building a new house. For the basic construction, contractors were hired, but most of the interior was designed and completed by Mike himself. A horseshoe-shaped driveway was convenient for exiting and entering because the four-bedroom house faced a busy street. On the first floor a large eat-in kitchen, a formal dining room, a laundry room, and a living room that opened onto a wraparound balcony, that faced the side and rear of the house and led to the backyard, were spacious and comfortable. A door from the kitchen was an entranceway to the two-car garage. Upstairs were the bedrooms. A Jacuzzi, a shower, a regular toilet, and bidet were featured in the huge master bathroom adjacent to the master bedroom. Indirect lighting, a laundry shoot, and a built-in safe were other special additions. The basement comprised the exercise room, a full kitchen, and a playroom with a door leading to the backyard.

The house was an ideal home for a new baby daughter, Chloe Alexis Picart. My first granddaughter was born on April 12, 1989 by caesarean section at Hackensack Hospital. Lori and Chloe were fine, but when Mike saw the surgeon operating on his beloved wife, he passed out and hit the edge of the table causing a gash on his forehead. The doctor had more trouble patching his wound than the entire caesarean section. Experiencing horrible emergency medical situations in Vietnam, Mike explained, "Seeing my love bleeding was too much to bear."

Mike and Lori mended well, and all the family bestowed their love and attention to an adorable, little girl. One of many fond memories of Chloe was the time I played Santa Claus at a Christmas party for the children and grandchildren of Elk members. Chloe would cry hysterically whenever her parents tried to sit her on Santa's lap for a photograph. When Chloe attended the Elks' party, Lori did not take a camera along because she had assumed that Chloe would never go to Santa. To everyone's pleasant surprise, she walked by herself right to me, sat on my lap, and told me what she wanted for Christmas. She never cried, but smiled through the whole conversation. Never calling me grandpa, I knew she had not recognized me and truly thought that I was Santa. I was elated, and Lori was amazed.

On Friday evenings at the Paramus Elks Lodge, a social night was held. The dance music and a buffet attracted a large number of members to attend this fun event. It was customary for one officer to be scheduled as a host for the evening, welcoming members and guests. The officer was also responsible for the recitation of the "Eleven O'Clock Toast," dedicated to absent members. As a Loyal Knight, I would take a turn to host for the evening, and at one of the Friday night gatherings, Eddie and his wife introduced me to their friend, Toni, an attractive widow from Woodcliff Lake. That night I asked her to dance, and it was the beginning of a relationship that lasted about seven years. Finding a dancing partner and a lady who enjoyed attending the numerous Elks' functions and mingling with my friends at first filled me with contentment. We enjoyed one another's company, but something was missing and the relationship did not last.

Joining the Elks was not only a way to volunteer, but also a means to meet and befriend a multitude of men and women. All Elks followed the order's mission to be helpful citizens and to believe in God. I participated with joyful exuberance for ten years, working diligently on various committees and fulfilling service for five years as a trustee, three years as chaplain, one year as Loyal Knight, and another as Leading Knight. Then in February of 1989, I was elected as Exalted Ruler of Paramus Elks Lodge #2001 and was officially installed in March, two weeks before Chloe was born.

In June 1989 at the New Jersey State Elks Convention in Wildwood, I won the first place award as the "Best Exalted Ruler." Instead of marching in the color guard at the New Jersey State Elks Convention parade, I strutted proudly behind the color guard directly in front of the marching members. It was exciting to be chosen the best out of a hundred thirty-nine Exalted Rulers. Nineteen eighty-nine was the beginning of my advancement in Elkdom.

Running the Paramus Elks Lodge with over seven hundred and fifty members was like being the president of a company. The workers, however, were volunteers. They received personal gratification instead of monetary rewards for their dedicated time and talents to promote various programs instituted by the Grand Lodge located in Chicago. As the Exalted Ruler, my duties of presiding over bi-monthly lodge meetings, overseeing the progress of various committees, attending district and state meetings, and raising funds for charitable commitments were demanding. The ultimate reward of my work with Elks resulted in long-term friendships with men and women, joining forces in the true meaning of the Brotherhood of Elks. The completion and success of each mandated program confirmed my belief in the positive benefits of teamwork and the goodness of mankind.

Performing in the ritual contests was another experience that enhanced my self-esteem, especially in the area of public speaking. Though I always seemed to communicate readily in English, I always found that the correct pronunciation of many English words was most difficult. Short vowels and certain letter combinations like "th" and "wh" are still troublesome. At times it was obvious that English was definitely not my first language. I persevered because I believed in the words I memorized and recited their meaning more than mere enunciation. In fact, my recommendation to upcoming officers is to recite the meaning of each passage, making memorization and recitation easier.

Elks combine work with lots of fun and laughter. Once a fundraiser was scheduled, crews of people would spend an entire weekend decorating, cooking, serving, and finally cleaning up. Chairing the committee planning Oktoberfest was one of my favorite fundraisers. I would get to wear my lederhosen. Since I love to cook, I would also assist the members on the kitchen committee with the preparation of authentic German food. Many ethnic parties celebrating other nationalities like Italian, Irish, and Polish were popular sellouts. Hawaiian Night, another dinner-dance I chaired, involved hiring a Hawaiian group performing their native dances and songs. Car shows, singing groups from the 1960s like "The Elegants," New Year's Eve dances, and family picnics were some of the special events to promote camaraderie and raise money for Elks' charities.

One of the most distinguished Elks' projects is Camp Moore known as "Miracle on the Mountain." The camp is located off of Route 287 in Haskell, New Jersey. The facility was entirely built and refurbished by Elks from all lodges in the state for the benefit of handicapped children. A specially constructed swimming pool, equipped with lifts, dormitory-like cabins, a dining hall with a complete kitchen, and recreational areas are provided for our "special kids." Elk lodges throughout the state sponsor and fund the admission for hundreds of applicants. Paying admission fees for the children attending Camp Moore's summer program is costly, but each week approximately one hundred children enjoy all sorts of activities free of charge. A counselor is assigned to each child and a full medical staff is on call at all times. It is heartwarming to note that the Elks from New Jersey are among the top contributors in the nation for charitable works and monetary donations.

Helping disabled veterans from the American Armed Forces is another proud commitment. Members of the Paramus Elks Lodge schedule visits to the Paramus Veterans Home bringing care packages filled with requested items. Special lunches and events at the lodge are also provided. Elks live the motto, "So long as there are veterans, the Benevolent and Protective Order of Elks will never forget them!"

Other commitments for every Elk lodge are the establishment of programs to benefit the youth in our communities in the area of drug awareness, Americanism, and scholarship awards based on scholastic achievement, good citizenship, and financial needs. The efforts made are countless, and benefits are appreciated.

After serving a year as Exalted Ruler, I continued my involvement in Paramus Elks Lodge's activities, but also expanded my work as chairman of the membership committee on the district level, and co-chairman of government relations on the state level.

On March 6, 1993, my services as an Elk were recognized at a gala dinner-dance that was given in honor of my election as "Elk of the Year" at Paramus Elks Lodge. My family attended the party. It was a proud occasion for me! An inscribed plaque, an Elk watch, an Elk of the Year lapel pin, along with other gifts from family and friends were presented to me for my year as an Elk. As customary, part of the evening festivities was a roast dedicated to the honored Elk of the Year. Most memorable was the "live" chicken popping out of the box, and a skit depicting my service in the French Foreign Legion with Joe and Pat tucked underneath the costume of a camel (I am not sure who was in the front or the back), and Bud and Don dressed as legionnaires. The evening of fun and laughter was a typical example of camaraderie and mutual respect Elks bestow on one another. I was most gratified to be among the very "Best People on Earth" (B.P.O.E), standing for the Benevolent and Protective Order of Elks!

After visiting a girlfriend who lived in Maryland, Carmen liked the area and decided to move there. While working as a paralegal secretary in a law firm, she enrolled in Essex Community College and eventually graduated with a bachelor of arts degree from Towson University in 1991. She purchased a townhouse in White Marsh and joined a ski club where she met Robert, a native of Baltimore. About a year later Carmen and Robert were married on October 2, 1993, at the Harrison Hotel at the Inner Harbor at Pier 5 in Baltimore. The outdoor ceremony with the view of the scenic harbor lighthouse provided a glorious background. As I escorted my beautiful daughter following the path between the rows of seated guests, I smiled proudly for her loving joy infused my mind and heart with happiness. Always level-headed with a positive outlook, Carmen left me with no doubts that her choices would lead to happiness and success. It is gratifying that both my children maintain confidence and determination in all aspects of their lives.

Sadly, thoughts that surfaced on Carmen's wedding day was that my parents were unable to attend. Father could have been there, but Mother was not well enough to travel, and of course, he would never attend without her. The following month, Mother had a stroke and died on December 26, 1993. They had been married sixty-seven years. Father died seven months later on July 6, 1994, two months before his one hundredth birthday. I visited Pop before I left for the Elks National Convention in Chicago, and his despondent words alarmed me. He voiced his displeasure about the modern television programs and music. He mentioned that all his friends, especially his beloved wife, had passed away, and he had little to look forward to in his daily existence. He seemed to be tired. I tried to cheer him, emphasizing that Alex and I were around and needed his good advice. When I left he seemed to be in better spirits. On the last day of the Elks' convention, I was notified that Father had passed away during an afternoon nap. Realizing that our last conversation was preparing me with the inevitable, I was sad and accepted the fact that Pop had departed peacefully without pain and had reunited with Mom. My heart swells with love and my mind thinks of respect for my ideal parents, who were also the ideal couple.

Advancing further in Elkdom, I was elected as state vice president of the northeast district and installed at the New Jersey State Convention in June of 1994. My major responsibility was to verify that each of the thirteen lodges in my district conformed to the Grand Lodge programs. Visiting each lodge, scheduling and overseeing the district meetings, and reporting at state meetings was time consuming. I was still employed at Lucas, but not traveling as much. On those occasions when Elk business conflicted with work, my boss would take my place on source inspections. The company appreciated my loyalty and dedication. It was mutual, for I loved my job but also loved being an Elk officer.

In November, when I learned that Lucas might sell their aerospace division, I decided that as soon as I reached ten years of service and my pension was vested, I would be eligible to retire. In March of 1995, I submitted my resignation, allowing a month for the company to hire a replacement. A week before retiring, the company invited me and my fellow employees to a farewell dinner-party. Speeches, gifts, and lots of best wishes for a happy retirement were given in my honor. Leaving co-workers who had become like family was difficult, but I also realized that at the age of sixty-eight, I was ready to retire. I wanted to devote more time as an Elk, and I did. I was appointed as district chairman for the convention parade and state chairman for memorial services, as well as chairman for Paramus Elks Lodge's renovation. Devoting more time to the Elks was most rewarding.

Retirement did not mean I would be slowing down. Even though I was no longer actively involved with the police reserves, I continued membership with the Tri-County Police Pistol League. Since the Wayne Police Team was short one man, I volunteered to fill the position, competing against my brother Alex who was a member of the Tenafly Pistol Team. At the end of the season, an awards dinner-dance was held, and even though I usually sat with Alex and his wife Arline, attending functions without a female companion was no fun. Occasionally, Arline or my friends' wives would ask me to dance, and I would politely oblige, but it was not the same as having a steady partner. Trying to be matchmakers, some of my friends arranged dates for me. Their efforts were appreciated, but with no positive results, until the year 1996 when my love life completely changed.

Unexpectedly, I became reacquainted with Judy who also tried to be a matchmaker. She introduced me to her aunt, and once again I felt the same, a lovely lady, but no spark. My dear friends Wayne and Wilma had introduced me to Judy and her husband Tom in 1976. We were all part of a group of friends living in Saddle Brook who were active with the police reserves and the Paramus Elks. We mingled at parties, dinner-dances, conventions, and other outings, including personal events. Judy and Tom attended my son's wedding and they invited me to their daughter's high school graduation party in 1993. I recall Judy complimenting my dancing skills, especially the Peabody, but we had never danced together. Admiring her dedicated and loving jobs as a mother and teacher, our friendship was mutual respect. I had seen Judy and Tom at several Elk events and occasionally around town but had not been in contact with them for nearly a year.

In August of 1996, I and other friends from Saddle Brook were invited to the twenty-fifth anniversary party for Wilma and Wayne. When Wayne told me that Judy and Tom would not be joining the celebration party because they had separated, I was as shocked as everyone else. I learned that Tom had moved out and was living with another woman, but Judy was still residing in their Saddle Brook house. Wilma confided that Judy's cousin Marge and Aunt Kitty were helping her to cope with the break-up of her twenty-eight year marriage.

Empathizing with Judy, her problems were a flashback to my failed marriage, so when she and her mother Rose invited me to dinner, I readily accepted. I was willing to offer my assistance if needed. Knowing one another for many years made it easy for all of us to chat about old times, our families, and the present situation.

Later, I learned that Michael, Judy's brother, who lived in Florida, offered to have their eighty-eight-year-old mother live with him. Judy was thankful for Michael's assistance. She would have more time to concentrate on herself and plan for the future. Judy was alone in the four-bedroom house, since her Mom was in Florida and her daughter was away at college. We would phone one another, not only to chat, but also to make sure that everything was all right. Months past by and our friendship was growing. It seemed that there would be no reconciliation between Judy and Tom. When I asked Judy out to dinner and dancing at The Crow's Nest, she accepted. We talked, danced, and laughed comfortably! Spotting an acquaintance from the pistol team, I introduced Judy. Being together seemed as natural as drinking water. Though I relished the feeling, I became anxious and admitted to my friend Wayne, "I think I am falling in love with Judy." We discussed my main concern, the difference in our ages; Judy was fifty and I was sixty-nine.

Wayne's advice, "Follow your heart and go for it!" I took his advice but would proceed slowly.

I invited Judy to the Elks New Year's Eve party, but she regretfully declined because of plans previously made to be with her cousin and aunt. Disappointment did not deter my efforts to patiently pursue the woman I loved. In April, Judy invited me to a birthday party for one of her colleagues, enabling me to become acquainted with her school friends. They seemed to be encouraging our friendship. Stephanie graduated from Rutgers University in May, moved back home, and started working in New York City. Celebrating Mother's Day with Stephanie, Judy, and cousin Marge and her family was another special way to get to know her family better. Everyone was getting accustomed to seeing Judy and me as a couple.

The ultimate event occurred in June of 1997, when Marge, Aunt Kitty, and Judy met me at the Elks Convention in Wildwood, spending three days together. Acquainted with most of the Elk members and their families at the local level, Judy felt comfortable. Judy was my date at the Elks State Ball, where I had the pleasure of introducing her to the Elks and their spouses at the New Jersey State level. Gloria, the wife of a past state president, already knew Judy since they worked together in the Wood-Ridge School District. Judy had taught Gloria's grandchildren who also lived in Wood-Ridge. Dancing to nearly every tune, happiness filled my heart. My friends were delighted to see me in high spirits.

Familiar with the charitable works accomplished by the Elks and the enjoyable activities, Judy had no trouble fitting in with the conventioneers. One of the highlights of the convention was the five-hour New Jersey State Elks Parade on Saturday afternoon. Unfortunately, the unseasonably cold and windy weather was not conducive to watching a parade, but Judy did convince Aunt Kitty and Marge to join her near the reviewing stand. She photographed the Paramus marchers, particularly the color guard and me as the captain. No matter the weather, it was a grand convention!

Since Judy had the summer off and had never been to Chicago, Illinois, she accepted my invitation to attend the Elks National Convention in July of 1997. We stayed with the New Jersey State contingent at the Sheraton Hotel overlooking the Chicago River's scenic view. Besides enjoying the numerous events sponsored by the Elks, we toured the Navy Pier, riding the enormous Ferris wheel. We took a boat ride on the Chicago River through the downtown area and the controlled locks connecting the canal to Lake Michigan. The expensive stores on the Magnificent Mile, the Elks National Memorial and Headquarters, and Michael Jordan's Restaurant were other attractions we toured. My life was energized and headed in a wonderful direction because I had fallen head over heals in love. Judy's feelings seemed to be mutual. Returning home, I shredded my application to the Elks Retirement Home in Virginia, for I was sure I would no longer be using it.

One evening during the summer, Mike and Lori invited Judy and me for dinner. They were attempting to get to know her better, and Judy would be doing the same. Her teacher instincts attract her to children, so meeting and talking to Chloe, my eight-year-old granddaughter, was especially warm and friendly. Acceptance and approval of our relationship were not only emanating from my family's eyes, but also evident by their cordial, loving manner. Just as important was Judy's comfortable demeanor with each of them.

In November of 1997, I purchased a one-bedroom apartment at the Park East Terrace Cooperative Apartments, in Paterson, and exactly two miles from Judy's house. Several of my friends, who are also Elks, live at Park East Terrace and recommended the facility. Mike organized a renovation of my apartment. He reworked the electric, built a custom-made wall unit in the living room, installed new light fixtures and kitchen cabinets, and put a drop ceiling in the bathroom. We worked together on most of the projects, but Mike handled the more difficult ones, not wanting me to overdo. He is and always will be a generous, caring son.

Judy and I delayed meeting Carmen and Robert until they were settled into their new home in Bel Air, Maryland. When we did visit, we spent the weekend in their center-hall colonial-style house, with four bedrooms, formal living and dining rooms, huge eat-in kitchen with an island counter, sunken family room, and a sunroom, adjacent to an outside deck with stairs leading down to a huge backyard that borders a state park. The house was part of a new development in a lovely neighborhood. Our visit was important for achieving closeness was our goal. Judy presented them with a custom-made floral arrangement as a housewarming gift. Carmen and Robert were delighted. Since Carmen had worked for a law firm in Wood-Ridge where Judy had been teaching for almost thirty years, they found common topics to discuss.

It was gratifying that Judy felt as comfortable with my family as I did with her family. Stephanie smiled whenever she saw us together. When we spent Easter of 1998 in Bradenton, Florida, with Judy's brother Michael and her mother Rose, we felt loving acceptance. Both our families were united in our happiness and approved our togetherness!

During the June Elks State Convention in 1998, I presented Judy with a friendship ring inscribed with the date 06-04-97, representing the day at the previous Elks Convention when I knew I had fallen in love. We attended the Elks National Convention in Anaheim, California in July, and then spent over a month with Michael and Rose in Bradenton. Cherished remembrances of leisurely days at Holmes Beach, on Anna Maria Island, gourmet dinners cooked by either Judy or me, dancing and dining at the Bradenton Elks Lodge, shopping excursions, and other family outings, confirmed the fact that I had found my true paradise in Florida.

Warnings of an upcoming hurricane that was targeted for the east coast and heading north caused Judy and me to leave Florida sooner than planned.

Judy wanted to be back in time to prepare for the first day of school. On Monday morning, August 24, 1998, after breakfast, Judy asked her mom to sit for a photograph to finish the role of film in the camera, but Rose refused. Judy assumed it was because she was still wearing her pajamas and bathrobe, but it seemed strange for Rose rarely hesitated to be in a picture. No amount of encouragement could change her mind. We thought she might be sad about us leaving. Kissing and hugging me, Rose said, "Take care of my little girl." Rose and her son planned to fly to New Jersey in September for her nintieth birthday party. Invitations had been sent to family and friends for a joyous birthday reunion.

That evening while Michael was watching Monday night football on television, Rose awoke from her sleep, walked into the living room and told her son she did not feel well. Rose passed away in Michael's arms. An aneurysm had burst in one of her arteries. The shocking news was hard to believe! Judy and I felt thankful and blessed to have been given the opportunity to spend a special time together with Mom in the summer of 1998.

Judy was officially divorced in May of 1999. Our commitment to one another grew even stronger in our hearts and mind. I did not think my life could become any happier, until the day in June when Judy accepted my engagement ring. Wanting to wait until Judy would retire from teaching, possibly in 2001, we decided not to set a date for a wedding until then.

During the summer of 1999, we attended another New Jersey State Elks Convention and in July the Elks National Convention in Kansas City, Missouri. Its twin city, Kansas City, Kansas, is directly opposite on the Kansas and Missouri Rivers. Visiting Independence, Missouri was most memorable, especially the President Harry S Truman House and Library and another museum depicting the history of the pioneers heading west in the Conestoga wagons. Purchasing items including a replica of the covered wagon, photographs, and a few books, Judy planned to use them to enrich her classroom instruction. Most interesting was the "tornado in a bottle," a popular selling item, because Kansas and Missouri were part of an area in the United States known as "tornado alley." When the blue-colored liquid in the container was swirled around, it would form a funnel-shape looking exactly like a tornado. Judy could not wait for her students to see the mini-tornado inside the bottle.

Celebrating the second millennium, New Year's Eve 2000, was not only special because Judy and I had been dating for two and a half years and engaged for six months, but also because I was appointed as District Deputy Grand Exalted Ruler. I was elated and looking forward to being installed at the Elks National Convention in Dallas, Texas. My jubilation enthusiastically spread to Judy, so much so, that she did not want to be introduced as my fiancée at the convention, but as my wife. We decided to marry before our trip in July.

In five months, we planned a lovely ceremony, held at the Paramus Elks on Saturday, June 25, 2000, with about eighty friends and family members in attendance. Judy's brother gave her away. Alex was my best man and Mike was an usher, escorting Stephanie, a bridesmaid. Marge was the maid-of-honor and Chloe was the flower girl. Carmen and Lori recited readings from the Bible and the minister's words still echo in my head, "I now pronounce you man and wife," followed by booming cheers and loud clapping. Alex and Arline alternated videotaping the festivities. Alex, using his professional camera, took many pictures that were compiled into a magnificent wedding album and video.

The next day, Mike hired a limousine to drive Alex, Arline, Judy, and me to the Chart House Restaurant on the Hudson River for a lovely dinner. Drinking champagne in the limo and chatting incessantly about the fun we had had at the wedding, we seemed to arrive quickly at the restaurant. Our conversation continued about Alex and Arline's move to Arizona. They reminisced about their years of living in Bergenfield, yet were delighted to be fulfilling a dream, for Alex always loved being a "cowboy" in the west. Their mutual and confirmed commitment to proceed on this new venture was obviously mixed with feelings of sadness to be moving far away from family and friends. Always thoughtful and most generous, my son and daughter-in-law planned this special outing not only as a tribute to my marriage, but also as a fond farewell for Alex and Arline.

The memories of that farewell dinner are cherished dearly. Alex and I realized that the two of us could still be close and caring of one another no matter how many miles separate us. Alex and Aline would be missed, but Judy and I had already arranged to visit them in Anthem after attending the convention in Dallas in July. The second millennium started a renewed personal life for the Picart brothers.

Being installed as the District Deputy Grand Exalted Ruler of the Northeast District from New Jersey at the Dallas Convention Center was the highlight of my Elks career. Judy was by my side at all the events to support my efforts to advance the programs mandated by the Grand Lodge throughout my year of service. Appointing four outstanding Elks: Richard, the secretary; Dave, auditor; Jack, assistant secretary; and John, esquire; as part of my team, also contributed to a successful year. Many accomplishments were approved and commended by the Grand Lodge.

My favorite duty as District Deputy was visiting each lodge to view and congratulate the officers for the rendition of the ritual in my honor and to praise the members for the completion of the planned activities for veterans, handicapped children, drug awareness, youth activities, scholarships, and all other implemented programs. My schedule was full. I was thankful to be retired and able to dedicate quality time to my duties as District Deputy Grand Exalted Ruler.

Even though I continued to maintain the one bedroom cooperative apartment in Paterson, Judy and I found it easier to live in her house in Saddle Brook. Stephanie lived with us. We all settled into an easy-going family life style.

In June of 2001 after thirty-three years of teaching, Judy decided to retire, leaving with wonderful memories and numerous accomplishments. The Veterans Day Program that received the New Jersey State Best Practices Award, Read-a-Thons, a school-wide play, "New Jersey's the Place for Me," visitations from authors, teacher-in-charge, were programs that made Judy proud. Several parents, the faculty, and every class participated in an assembly program to present surprises honoring Judy, as the "heart" of Catherine E. Doyle School. A slide show, original songs, and a gigantic album were amazing tributes. A special dinner-dance held at the Wayne Manor, attended by colleagues, friends, and family was also especially heartwarming. I was given a fedora to wear and Judy was draped in a red cape, her favorite color. We were escorted to designated seats to be entertained by the Doyle staff, performing a skit and singing the main song, "The Lady Is a Champ." We were then asked to dance the jitterbug to one of our favorite songs, "In the Mood." Speeches were made, resulting in lots of tears and cheers, hugs and kisses, and smiles and laughter. It was a glorious evening with a final dance, a waltz, to our wedding song, Ann Murray's hit, "Can I Have This Dance for the Rest of My Life?" During our dance, Judy whispered into my ear, "I fall in love with you more and more every time we dance." We dance often!

My special retirement gift to Judy was a gold charm of Jesus, inscribed with the years 1968-2001 on the back. Ironically, the retirement dinner-dance was on Ascension Thursday, a holy day, so my gift was most meaningful to Judy, a faithful Roman Catholic. She and I continue to attend Sunday Mass, singing in the church choir. We love being together. It is natural to explore one another's interests and hobbies, yet with respect for one another's independence.

Happy and good times seem to whiz by quickly, and before I knew it, Judy and I were celebrating our first wedding anniversary, June 25, 2001. That September, we were invited to her cousin's fiftieth wedding anniversary on September 8. Mike arrived from Florida to join the festivities for cousins Pat and Dolores. Renewing their vows before family and friends was a loving inspiration for all married couples. Joyful family gatherings are priceless.

Unfortunately, three days later on Tuesday, September 11, 2001, our joyful memories were replaced with horrid visions of hijacked airplanes. Terrorists had attacked the World Trade Center in New York City and the Pentagon in Washington, DC. As Judy and I were sitting down to eat breakfast, the events unraveling on the television seemed unreal. At first, we thought that the first plane had accidentally crashed into the tower. A news alert transferred the regular broadcaster to the voice of a reporter interviewing a witness, who continually insisted, "I saw a jumbo jet, not a small plane, crash into the tower."

The reporter's tone seemed to be doubtful of the witness's statement and once again rephrased his question, "Tell us exactly, what did you see?"

The excited and desperate man repeated unwavering in a strong voice, "It was a jet that turned and headed right into the tower!" We soon learned that the collision was deliberate, for we watched a second plane crash into the second tower.

For fifty years, cousins Pat and Dolores have lived in Weehawken, a small town in Hudson County, New Jersey, overlooking the Hudson River and downtown New York City. They tearfully watched the twin towers collapse and vanish from sight. We found out later that Michael's Continental Airlines flight from Newark Airport to Tampa took off at eight twenty , before the attack on the first tower. His plane landed safely and on time in Florida. Stephanie, who usually drives over the George Washington Bridge to her job on East 87th Street, did not go to work on Tuesday, but thousands of commuters from New Jersey who were in New York City that day will never be the same. Many individuals, who were personally impacted by the horrors of 9/11, may never recover.

With the passing of time, it might seem as if the public has become complacent, returning to life's inevitable chores and responsibilities. Perhaps falling into step and refocusing on mundane routines may bring comfort to many, enabling minds to cope with tragedies. I believe we should try to live our lives completely and fully without succumbing to the fear of terrorism; however, we should never forget what happened on 9/11 and be more alert to any strange and unusual behavior. Cooperating with authorities, patiently adhering to more stringent searches at airports, passing through machines to detect weapons, or complying with any other procedure to enhance safety should be welcomed by all. Many Americans may not like the restrictions, but most of us will adapt to the necessary precautions. Others unfortunately may never feel safe anywhere, no matter what is required. Trusting in God and appreciating every day of my life have been my ways to cope and move forward

Greg, Stephanie's boyfriend, surprised her with an engagement ring in January of 2002. She accepted, and they were married on Valentine's Day, February 14, 2004. Judy and I were gloriously happy for them. After

Stephanie and Greg bought Judy's house, we moved permanently to my co-op apartment in Paterson.

Stephanie was not the only one whose life was changing. Events in my life in 2002 were like a relay race starting with the initial event, attending the centennial celebration at Tampa Elks Lodge #708. Judy and I were part of a delegation of Elks from New Jersey invited to this special occasion. Several of our Elk friends were "snow birds," living part of the time in Florida, which sounded like a good idea to us. Our neighbors in Paterson and also a couple at the centennial celebration, Fran and John lived part time in Florida. They invited us to their home in Hudson, a town north of Tampa, and showed us around the area with a special dinner in Tarpon Springs. Staying at their home for a few days gave us the opportunity to contact a realtor and to check out the condominiums for sale, but unfortunately we did not find any property that attracted our attention. We headed south to Bradenton to visit with my brother-in-law Michael and share with him our interest in possibly purchasing a condominium in his area.

Before we had a chance to contact a realtor, we were invited to visit a fellow member of the Paramus Elks and his wife who also resided in Bradenton in the Ironwood-Pinebrook section. Driving east on Cortez Road into the main entrance, I made a right turn onto Pinebrook Circle passing three condominium buildings and pink villas. Realizing I was heading the wrong way, I wanted to make a U-turn, but Judy said, "There's a sign, 'Villa for sale by owner,' with a phone number."

Since we were curious about which villa was for sale, Judy used her cell phone and called the number. A man answered, explaining that his wife was at villa #4 with a prospective buyer and that it would be all right to stop by. After exiting the car, we followed the path into a small courtyard, beautifully landscaped with hibiscus bushes, a palm tree, and other flowers. The owner showed us around. We were pleasantly surprised to see a spacious apartment that included a large kitchen with a nook for a table and chairs, an adjacent laundry room, and a door leading to the oversized garage. There was a small hallway leading to a guest bedroom with a private bath and closets. Then facing the west side of the villa, we walked through the large master bedroom with a private bath, powder room, and a large walk-in closet. In addition, an open area that could be furnished as a living room and dining room was spacious. French doors to a step-down enclosed lanai overlooked a man-made pond and the eighth hole on the golf course. Judy and I loved the layout of the villa and conveyed our interest in the property to the owner. After further discussion, we took a short walk to the Pinebrook clubhouse, a facility used by the owners of the condominiums and the villas. We toured the heated pool, a Jacuzzi, a well-equipped exercise room, a dance studio, art workshop, a room with a pool table, another room with a ping-pong table, a small library, a sitting room with a television and piano, and a large entertainment hall with a kitchen. We knew that investing in the Villas at Pinebrook would be perfect for us.

Michael had lived in Bradenton for over twenty years and agreed with our choice that the property was superb. The deal was finalized in March of 2002, when we returned to paint, decorate, and furnish the villa. We returned to New Jersey for Stephanie and Greg's engagement party and our previously arranged trip to Hawaii. My life was truly running on high speed. I did not mind for I was able to keep up with all the happenings.

Flying non-stop from Newark to Honolulu, Judy and I boarded the Norwegian Star, a brand new cruise ship. It was Judy's first cruise. From Honolulu we sailed to Hilo, stopping for a shore excursion at the Kilauea volcano. The next stop was Fanning Island in the Republic of Kiribati that was located two hundred twenty-eight miles north of the Equator. Since the Norwegian Star is not an American ship, it must dock in a foreign port before returning to the Hawaiian Islands in America, so one day a week, the passengers are treated to swim and picnic on the island. We purchased handcrafted items made by the natives, who also entertained us with songs and dances. Fanning Island is about twenty-six square miles and on the west side of the International Date Line. We spent May 8 on the island and that evening we crossed over the date line and back to May 7. It was an unusual experience.

Continuing the cruise, the ship headed north and stopped at Maui, where we joined fellow passengers at a Polynesian luau. We ate roasted pig, sweet potatoes, and poi, a staple vegetable for the Hawaiians. Poi is made from the taro root and blended with other ingredients into a pasty texture. It tasted bland and needed to be eaten with the other spicy or sweet delicacies to give it some flavor.

Falling in love with the friendly Hawaiian people was easy for us. The Hawaiian Islands and especially the music and dances were romantically beautiful. Learning the hula and a dance to the "Hukilau" was lots of fun. We performed the dances on stage. Judy and the other women wore Hawaiian dresses and several men including me were chosen to wear authentic Tahitian attire. After the performances, our instructor presented each of us with certificates proclaiming, "Hula Mastery." Dancing the Tahitian War Dance was too much for me. The next day I wound up in the ship's infirmary, where the doctor diagnosed a sprained knee. I spent the rest of the day relaxing in the Jacuzzi, instead of touring the island of Kauai.

Returning to Honolulu, Oahu on Mother's Day, Sunday, May 12, Judy and I disembarked and boarded a bus to the Ocean Resort Hotel, one block from Waikiki Beach. An exotic floral arrangement with a bottle of champagne including glasses and snacks were on the table in our hotel room. They were sent from Stephanie and Greg in honor of Mother's Day! Later that evening, we dined at the Honolulu Elks Lodge #616 on Waikiki Beach with a magnificent view of Diamond Head. Every mother was presented with a long-stemmed rose. Though we were not with our children, it was a most memorable Mother's Day.

The next day we toured Pearl Harbor and the USS *Arizona* Memorial. The wreckage of the battleship submerged under the water with bubbles of oil still leaking to the surface was a somber view. Hundreds of sailors were entombed in the ship since the attack on December 7, 1941. We continued the tour to the Memorial Cemetery of the Pacific with over thirty thousand graves located within the Punchbowl Crater. These memorials are significant and remind us of the ultimate sacrifice for freedom. Our remaining days in Honolulu were spent visiting the zoo, the aquarium, shopping at the market places, swimming, and relaxing on Waikiki Beach. Judy and I loved our vacation but were anxious to return to Bradenton and complete the decorating and furnishing of the villa. We finished in time for Stephanie and Greg's visit over the Thanksgiving holiday in November of 2002.

The Bradenton/Sarasota area has been labeled as one of the best places for retirees because of the many activities available to satisfy every whim. Theaters for plays and symphonic performances, many golf courses, extensive beaches, art and history museums, a new planetarium, and a few Elk lodges are nearby. I became an associate member of the Bradenton Elks Lodge #1511 with over thirteen hundred members. It is a beautiful lodge with an in-house caterer, providing lunches and dinners, with live musicians or karaoke two or three times a week, a pool with a tiki bar, and lots of marvelous Elks. Judy and I frequently patronize the lodge and have made many friends for we love to socialize and dance. We also joined the St. Joseph Church and choir, singing at the eleven o'clock Mass each Sunday morning with a group known as the Celebrity Singers. Practicing each Tuesday for our performance on Sundays, holidays, and special events is fun because the members and directors are delightful.

Living at the Villas at Pinebrook has enabled us to become members of the social club and to attend monthly meetings and fun-filled parties. We are also learning how to golf, since the golf course is in the center of the Ironwood-Pinebrook community and easy for us to access. Golfing is not easy. While sitting comfortably in our lanai, we have observed many golfers sinking balls into our pond instead of into the hole. Using an extended wand with a hooked cup attached to the bottom, they try to fish for their lost golf ball. I have often spent time retrieving my golf balls from the ponds. Golfing can be frustrating, yet Judy and I do not take the game too seriously. We are enjoying the exercise and camaraderie with fellow golfers. Line dancing, water aerobics, knitting, reading and joining two organizations, the Boa Sisterhood of America and the New Floridians, are other fun activities for Judy. We are happily busy, but our time in Bradenton gets even better when family and friends spend a vacation with us. In fact, one of my Elk friends, Bill and his wife Judy, visited and purchased the villa next door. I must admit that once you visit Bradenton, you may wind up like me and become pleasantly displaced to Florida. This time the word "displaced" has happy connotations.

In March 2005, we traveled with friends from Bradenton on a ten-day Royal Caribbean Cruise to the eastern Caribbean. The *Horizon* cruise ship left from the port of Tampa. We also traveled to Arizona in May to stay with Alex and Arline. Alex was not only our driver and tour guide on trips to Sedona and Las Vegas but also our personal photographer providing a detailed scrapbook and DVD disc of our entire vacation. I consider my younger brother a master craftsman in photography. His work can be compared to professionals.

For a few years, I have tried to set aside time to write about my life's experiences, but pleasant distractions have caused delays. In September of 2005, my son Mike was responsible for sparking my determination to finish my book. On my seventy-eighth birthday, Mike and his wife Lori, along with Chloe and her boyfriend, invited Judy and me to a birthday dinner at the Chart House on the Hudson River. It was a sunny, glorious evening with a crystal clear view of the New York skyline. Two cruise ships were heading out to the Atlantic Ocean. The site was magnificent. Before and after dinner, we posed for pictures that recorded the day's splendor. After that, Mike drove us on a tour of the new construction along the Hudson River. The office buildings and apartment complexes were constructed after the attack on the World Trade Center to satisfy the demand for more facilities. Since space was available on the New Jersey side of the Hudson River, towns like Jersey City, Hoboken, and Edgewater were revitalized. A scenic river walk was constructed for residents as well as rail service. We were amazed at the areas improvements. Investors truly envisioned a back up community across the river from Wall Street. Many towns in New Jersey are truly extensions of one of the world's greatest metropolis, New York City.

After our tour, we returned to Mike's house for another birthday surprise, a treasure chest with brass palm trees adorning the top and sides. I could not imagine what was inside the chest. I unlatched the hook and opened the lid to discover a *kepi blanc*, the white legionnaire's hat, which I immediately plopped on my head. I also saw an entire legionnaire's uniform.

I was completely amazed and confused! When I started taking the items out of the chest, I discovered all sorts of memorabilia associated with the French Foreign Legion packed inside. There were many precious objects: two Arabian daggers, towels with the Legion's logo, decals, an unopened bottle of wine made specifically for the legionnaires, several books, postcards, photographs, an ashtray, metal containers, canteen, holster and belt, and a complete uniform that unfortunately did not fit. Once again, photographs were taken and capture the shocking expression on my face when first seeing the birthday surprises.

Researching and purchasing each item on the international eBay, it took Mike over a year to fill the treasure chest. Mike's loving efforts were much appreciated, and the legionnaire memorabilia reminded me that finishing my book should be a priority. Once I returned to Florida, work would begin in earnest.

Unexpectedly, a week later Mike had major surgery with complications, and he nearly died. After several months, he was finally able to return to work. I will always be concerned about his condition and pray for him every day.

Making a positive effort, Judy assisted with the completion of my story. My life is content. I approach each day good-naturedly, assisting others whenever I can. The ultimate is sharing my life with my love, my friend, my wife Judy. She makes life happy.

Our children are our gifts. Each one is different and very dear and special, bringing much joy to me. Mike, Lori, and Chloe, who will be graduating from high school in June 2007, are finally happily residing in their new home. Carmen, Robert, and Maiya, who is finishing kindergarten in June 2007, are also happy and well. Carmen and Maiya visited China for a few weeks as part of a delegation volunteering to work in one of the orphanages. Maiya is truly a world traveler and our Chinese princess. Stephanie and Greg are happy, too. Greg is pursuing his interest in art and has graciously completed the illustration for my book's cover. He is a talented artist. Using oil paints, he reproduced *The Blue Madonna*, one of the many priceless art works we had seen at the Ringling Art Museum on their last visit. It is one of Judy's favorite paintings, so Greg surprised her with his rendition of this magnificent painting for Christmas. She cried upon seeing his beautiful gift. It hangs prominently over my Wurlitzer organ. Yes, I am trying to rekindle my love of playing the organ, and I practice as often as I can. Mastering the chords is a challenge. I rely more on my natural ability to play by ear than by the written notes.

My final thoughts reflect on two words—surprised and grateful. These two words have often been used to describe my feelings when experiencing the happenings throughout my life. I am grateful for many things, but I am especially thankful to be no longer labeled as a displaced person and truly appreciative to be living in the best country in the world. I am grateful that my life still encompasses surprises that cause me to feel like a child filled with excitement and expectations. I am also grateful for caring friends and family and God's blessings. I pray that His blessings continue for my children and my children's children. My advice to them is to cherish surprises and be grateful for the unlimited opportunities available in a free country. God bless my beloved country, the United States of America.

I thank God for every accomplishment, for the goodness He has bestowed on Judy and me, and for the completion of my life story.

A
Lifetime
of Memories

Photo Album

Grandfather Jon Pierre Picart,
Russian czarist officer

Grandmother Elisabeth Kulikowicz Picart

Captain Alexander Picart,
Father's oldest brother

Sergius Picart, my father,
at his graduation from military academy

Photographed at her wake, Grandmother Elisabeth
died at 103 years of age.

Fuchs family, 1917: my mother, Eugenie; Grandfather Otto;
Aunt Helena; Grandmother Emma; Aunt Olga; and Aunt Lida

Picart family, 1938: (bottom row) Mother, me, and Uncle Valentine;
(top row) Uncle George, Grandma Elisabeth, Aunt Tanya, and Father

Vilnius, 1939: With Mother, and Prince,
my pet Doberman

With Alex, 1943

With Father at Velejka River, Vilnius

Alex, early cowboy days, 1950

Alex, present day cowboy, 2006

Postcard of Sidi-Bel-Abbes, Algiers

In the French Foreign Legion, 1946

My birthday present of French Foreign Legion memorabilia
from Mike and Lori, 2005

Cousin Alexandria, Helena's daughter, in Australia

Linz, Austria, 1953: (bottom row) Alex and my brother-in-law George;
(top row) me; my mother-in-law, Anna, with Mike; my mother and father

As chief of the East Paterson Fire Auxiliary, 1960

Standing next to the Radiological Civil Defense Vehicle

On the way to march in the Memorial Day Parade
with Carmen and Mike in East Paterson

As captain of East Paterson Fire Department Color Guard

Paramus, 1965: Father and Mother

Father and Mother standing in front of a mural Father painted
of Kauai Beach for my new house in Paramus

Mother, Mike and Father

As Captain of Paramus Police
Reserves, 1973

Dressed up as a French sailor on
the cruise ship *Oceanic*, 1975

Alex and I at New Jersey State Elks Convention in Wildwood

Marching in a Fourth of July Parade as captain of Paramus Elks Color Guard

Father holding his great-granddaughter Chloe Alexis Picart, 1989

Judy's brother Michael and Rose, their mother, 1998

With Judy at an Elks function

My stepdaughter Stephanie and her husband, Greg, 2006

My china-doll granddaughter, Maiya Grace, 2006

My daughter Carmen and her husband, Robert, with Maiya, 2005

My son Mike and his wife, Lori, 2006

My granddaughter Chloe, 2007

Alex and his wife, Arline, 2007

Judy and I, in Florida, 2007

Printed in the United States
80433LV00006B/349-369